Predictive Analytics in 56 Minutes

Steven Finlay

iii

To Sam and Ruby.

CONTENTS

Forward   vii

1   Introduction   1

2   What is Predictive Analytics?   4

3   What Do the Scores Generated by a Predictive Model Represent?   7

4   Why Use Predictive Analytics. What Value Does it Add?   12

5   How Does Predictive Analytics Work?   15

6   Using a Predictive Model to Make Decisions   25

7   That's Scorecards, but What About Decision Trees?   29

8   Putting Predictive Analytics to Work   34

9   The Relationship Between Big Data and Predictive Analytics   45

10   Ethical Considerations   50

11   The Cutting Edge of Predictive Analytics   57

12   Concluding Remarks   66

Appendix A. Evaluating Predictive Models   67

Appendix B. Further Information and Recommended Reading   75

Appendix C. Popular Terms in Predictive Analytics   80

Forward

56 minutes. That's the time it takes my commuter train to travel from my home town of Preston to the great British city of Manchester. I find this to be an ideal time to catch up on a bit of reading.

Having written several "normal length" books about predictive analytics I thought that this would be a great title for a short introduction to this fascinating subject, which is having an ever increasing impact across many aspects of our lives.

The average person reads at about 250 words a minute. With 56 minutes to play with, that equates to about 14,000 words. Including preliminary matter and appendices the total length of the text is somewhat longer, but I hope that the average reader is able to digest the main part of the book in the allotted time.

1 Introduction

If you have a job, own a credit card, claim welfare benefits, pay taxes, use the internet or engage with any large consumer organization, then predictive analytics will be having an impact on your life in one way or another. This is because predictive analytics is the primary tool that organizations use to leverage the data they hold about you. Predictive analytics informs them about how you are likely to behave in different circumstances, and hence the way that they should deal with you in order to maximize their (and sometimes your) objectives.

This short text provides a managerial (i.e. non-technical, no assumptions about previous knowledge and no formulas) overview of predictive analytics, what it is and how it's used. To put it another way, if you can read and write and do a bit of basic arithmetic, then you should be OK with the material in this book. The topics covered in this text include:

- What predictive analytics is.
- What a predictive model looks like.
- The sort of things organizations use predictive analytics for.
- The relationship between predictive analytics and Big Data.
- The people and tools needed to do predictive analytics.
- How to apply predictive analytics to improve business processes and the bottom line.
- Legal and ethical issues when using predictive analytics.
- The pitfalls and limitations of predictive analytics.

A good question to ask at this point is: why do I need to know these things? One reason is personal. Predictive analytics is widely applied by organizations to decide how to treat you. They use it to decide if you will receive a great offer or a poor one, if you should be placed at the front or the back of the queue, if you will be subject to a tax audit or treated as a suspect in a criminal case. Therefore, it's not a bad idea to know something about it so that you can understand why an organization may have treated you in one way and not in another.

The other reason to learn about predictive analytics, and the one that is the main focus of this book, is that it is now a mainstream business tool. Not that long ago, predictive analytics was the domain of few nerdy specialists working mainly in financial services or large marketing departments. These days, anyone whose day-to-day role requires them to deal with people on a regular basis may come across it. This doesn't mean that you need to learn all the technical details that an analytics specialist (a data scientist) needs to know. However, having a working knowledge of what predictive analytics is and how it can be used to help organizations deliver better products and services will be beneficial. Not least, because in order to make effective use of predictive analytics, it needs to be focused on business needs.

To get the most out of predictive analytics, data scientists need to engage with business users to understand their problems. Data scientists also need to understand an organization's culture, and its approach to the adoption of new ideas, technologies and working practices. It doesn't matter how good a solution is in terms of cutting edge hardware and software, if it's not aligned with an organization's business objectives and operational processes, then it's all just a waste of time and money.

Lots of solution suppliers can bamboozle you with their fancy tech, but the ones that add value will be those that spend time to understand how you and your organization work. They will then determine if and how their predictive analytics solutions can be used to improve what you and your organization does.

Successful predictive analytics is a two way thing. Data scientists need to know something about the business, and the business needs to understand a little bit about predictive analytics. Without this joint understanding it's unlikely that an organization will be able to realize the full benefits that predictive analytics has to offer.

2 What is Predictive Analytics?

Predictive Analytics (PA) is the application of mathematics to analyze patterns in historic data, in order to be able to predict future behavior. It's a type of forecasting that seeks to find relationships (correlations) between past and future events[1]. You will hear terms like "Data mining", "Machine learning" "Artificial intelligence" and "Deep learning" being thrown about when people talk about predictive analytics, but it's all just different types of math at the end of the day.

A **predictive model** (or just model going forward) is the output generated by the predictive analytics process. The model captures the relationships between past and future behavior that have been discovered by the analytics. Once a model has been created, it can be used to generate new predictions about the future. Organizations then use the model's predictions to decide how to treat people.

There are lots of different types of predictive model, and there are dozens, if not hundreds, of mathematical techniques and algorithms that can be used to generate a model. However, regardless of the type of model or the mathematics used to create it, a model's predictions are almost always represented by a single number - a **score**. The higher the score the more likely someone is to behave in the way the model predicts, the lower the score the less likely they are to behave in that way.

One of the most familiar applications of predictive analytics is credit scoring. When someone wants a loan, credit card or mortgage, the lender asks the individual questions about themselves and their lifestyle. They then combine this with information from a credit report containing details about the individual's previous borrowing history, provided by a credit reference agency such as Experian or Equifax[2]. The information is then fed into a predictive model to generate a credit score. If you live in the USA, you will probably be familiar with FICO scores. A high FICO score (>750) is a prediction that someone is very likely to repay any money they borrow; i.e. they are creditworthy. A low score (<500) indicates that someone is very uncreditworthy. Banks and finance companies the world over use similar credit scoring methods.

Predictive analytics can be applied in all sorts of situations and to many types of problem, but most applications of predictive analytics relate to what people are going to do or how they will behave in the future, based on what you know about them today[3]. Another well-known application of predictive analytics is target marketing. Given information about someone's age, gender, income, web-browsing, purchase history and so on; a marketing department can predict if the person is interested in a particular product or not. They then use that prediction to decide whether or not to target them with promotional offers. Likewise, predictive models can also be used to infer how much people are willing to pay for products like insurance. This information is then used to tailor a personalized pricing strategy to each person's individual circumstances.

Another example of predictive analytics in action is preventative health care. Traditional health care systems are reactive. People seek medical assistance when they feel ill. Doctors then do their best to treat the illnesses they are presented with – which can be very costly and time consuming. These days, advanced heath care systems are increasingly focusing their attention on prevention rather than cure. This vastly reduces costs and improves patient outcomes. Predictive analytics is used to assess people's medical records and predict the likelihood of them developing specific conditions such as heart disease or diabetes, often years in advance. Those individuals that come at the top of the pile; i.e. those that the model predicts are most likely to get the disease, are then contacted with a view of initiating preventative action. For example, making lifestyle changes or prescribing preventative medication.

That's just a few applications of predictive analytics. Today, predictive analytics is being applied to a huge range of problems. In fact, almost any aspect of life that involves making decisions about large numbers of people. The algorithms that match people on dating sites, the technology used to detect credit card fraud, and systems for identifying terrorist suspects are all based on predictive analytics. If you want a more comprehensive list of applications then see the book by Eric Siegel[4], which details more than 120 different applications of predictive analytics in use today – and that's not a comprehensive list!

3 What Do the Scores Generated by a Predictive Model Represent?

Predictive models generate scores. These scores can be one of two types:

1. **Probability (likelihood) scores.** These predict specific events. Will someone do something or not? The technical name for a predictive model of this type is a **classification model.**

2. **Magnitude (quantity) scores.** These predict the amount of something. For example, how much someone will spend in store, or how long before they do something. The technical name for a predictive model of this type is a **regression model.**

Classification models predict *if* an event will occur, whereas regression models are concerned with the size, length or timing of events. Some common applications of classification models include:

• **Customer attrition.** The model score represents the probability that a customer will defect to a rival's product, or otherwise stop using a product or service. For example, switching their utility provider, acquiring a new credit card or cancelling a magazine subscription.

- **Medical diagnosis.** The score is a measure of the likelihood of someone having or getting a particular illness.

- **Credit card fraud.** The score generated by the model represents the probability that a card transaction is fraudulent.

- **Employment retention.** The score estimates the probability that an employee will leave their current position to take up another post.

- **Target marketing.** The scores represents the likelihood that someone will buy a given product or service.

Sometimes the scores from a classification model represent a probability directly. A person who receives a score of 0.0 certainly won't experience the event, while a score of 1.0 means that they certainly will.

Predictive models don't provide perfect predictions. What one tends to see is a spread (a distribution) of probabilities between 0.0 and 1.0 for individuals within the population. When a target marketing model generates a score of 0.70 for someone, this means that the model predicts that there is a 70% chance that the individual will buy the product or service and a 30% chance that they won't.

In other situations, the score from a classification model is transformed to a certain scale. Perhaps the best known example of this are credit scores, as discussed earlier. Credit scores tend to be scaled so as to range from about 400 to about 800[5]. If someone receives a score of 400, that means that they are very unlikely to repay any credit advanced to them (<5% chance that the loan will be repaid). A score of 800 means that they will almost certainly repay their debt (>99.9% chance that the loan will be repaid).

Regression models on the other hand are all about quantities; i.e. the magnitude of an event. Some example applications of regression models include:

- **Credit loss.** When someone defaults on a loan, how much of the debt is likely to be written-off?

- **Spend.** How much is someone likely to spend in their local supermarket in the next 12 months?

- **Life expectancy.** How long is a person expected to live?

- **Call length.** How long is a phone call predicted to last?

- **Response time.** How long after sending someone a letter, e-mail or text, does it take them to reply?

Sometimes the score from a regression model is a direct estimate of what one is trying to predict. A spend model that generates a score of 873 means that the customer is predicted to spend $873. In other situations, the score is scaled to represent percentiles, or to allocate a grade from 1 to 10 or similar. Grade 1 represents the very best (most profitable) customers, Grade 10 the least profitable.

Both regression and classification models are widely used, but classification models tend to be the most popular. This is because simple will they/won't they type customer events have traditionally been the easiest for organizations to understand. There also tends to be less ambiguity in how problems are defined, making it simpler for data scientists to translate business objectives into an appropriate numerical representation that the predictive analytics process can then be applied to.

What type of model to use (regression or classification) depends very much on what one wants to do with the model scores. If all I'm interested in is identifying which credit card customers are likely to attrite to a competitor's product, then what I need is a classification model to predict the probability of attrition. A retention strategy (such as offering a discount or free gift) is then applied to try to retain those customers most likely to defect to a rival; i.e. those with the highest scores.

If on the other hand, my primary concern is to identify profitable customers, with a view of encouraging them to spend more, than what I need is a regression model to predict who are going to be the big spenders and target those.

However, if I'm interested in retaining profitable customers who spend a lot on their cards, and I don't care about losing unprofitable customers who don't use their cards very much, then the best approach is to build two predictive models:

1.   An attrition model to predict those customers most likely to defect to a rival product (Classification).

2.   A revenue model to identify which customers spend the most (Regression).

The two models are then used in combination to drive a retention strategy as shown in Figure 1.

Figure 1. Using two models in combination.

		Probability of defecting to rival product (Score from attrition model)	
		Low	High
Estimated spend (Score from revenue model)	Low	Do nothing	Do nothing
	High	Do nothing	Apply retention strategy

By using the two models in combination, significant cost savings can be achieved. This is because resources aren't spent trying to retain customers that won't attrite, or those that have a high probability of attrition, but don't spend much on their cards.

Note that the models only provide predictions about what

customer's will do. They don't tell you what should then be done on the basis of those predictions. So with regards to what retention strategy should be applied to high spending customers that are likely to attrite, that's an additional consideration that an organization needs to address within the overall scope of a predictive analytics project. This is important because quite a common failing is for organizations to build some very good predictive models, and then not use them for anything. Making the right decisions and then acting upon those decisions is vital if a predictive analytics project is going to be successful.

4 Why Use Predictive Analytics. What Value Does it Add?

Predictive models are increasingly being used to replace and/or supplement expert judgement and manual decision making in all sorts of areas. This is because predictive models tend to be:

- **More accurate than human experts.** Predictive models sometimes get their predictions wrong just like people, but the overwhelming evidence is that on average, they don't get it wrong quite as often. In many fields, predictive models consistently outperform human experts by 20-30%; i.e. they make 20-30% fewer errors, or identify 20-30% better (more important/more profitable) cases.

- **Unbiased.** Unlike people, predictive models don't display prejudicial bias against people because of their gender, race, disability, etc. Don't get me wrong, models do display bias, but if a model tends to give certain individuals or groups higher or lower scores than the population at large, then this is based on hard statistical evidence – it's not based on some unfounded preconception or stereotype.

- **Fast.** As part of an automated decision making system, a predictive model can predict the behaviour of millions of people in seconds. In most cases it would be unfeasibly expensive and time consuming to have people manually making the same judgements.

- **Cheap**. Once developed, predictive models are often cheaper to deploy than their human counterparts.

In summary, predictive models can be used to make better, cheaper and faster decisions than those made by human experts. What this means is that in many areas predictive models are replacing people. In particular, white collar roles that require highly trained staff to use their expert judgement to decide what to do.

This is not a new phenomenon. In the 1950s and 1960s most applications for personal loans in the USA were assessed by human underwriters who individually reviewed each loan application. They then came to a decision as to whether or not that person was creditworthy and should therefore, get the loan they had applied for.

In large organizations, entire office buildings were taken up by underwriting teams who spent their days making lending decisions. In local bank branches, the Bank Manager was king – a respected member of the local community with absolute discretion over who could be given a loan or mortgage, and who could not.

By the late 1980s most of these roles were redundant. The role of bank managers had been reduced to little more than that of a salesperson – fronting the customer relationship, but having no decision making capability. The vast majority of lending decisions were being made by credit scoring models that sat at the heart of an automated decision making system located at head office. In the world of credit granting these days, only unusual or borderline cases tend to be reviewed by a human being – the vast majority of lending decisions are made without any human intervention at all.

Job losses are a concern for those in affected industries, but it's not all doom and gloom. In many cases predictive analytics is adding value to roles rather than supplanting them. In hospitals and doctors' surgeries, for example, predictive models supplement doctors' own judgement rather than replacing it. In marketing, improved targeting based on predictive analytics is used to reduce nuisance calls and junk mail, while at the same time maximizing worthwhile customer contacts; i.e. only phone/text/e-mail people who are very likely to be interested in what you are selling. In the past, blanket contact strategies were common. Staff in call centers would be supplied with phone books and told to work their way through them, calling as many people as they could regardless of their propensity to buy the product or service on offer. HR departments also make use of predictive analytics to pre-screen job applications, to remove those least likely to be suited to a given role. This allows HR staff to concentrate more of their time on the most promising prospects.

Another opportunity that predictive analytics makes possible is forecasting new types of behavior that were not considered or were not cost effective before. In policing for example, predictive models are helping police officers narrow down suspect lists and better target crime, improving efficiency and giving them more time to focus on the most serious crimes. Likewise, predictive models are fundamental to "people matching" services such as dating and job sites. Without predictive models these would be very different affairs – matching people based on a very crude set of criteria, and/or having to use people to do the matching, making such services very much more expensive and less efficient.

5 How Does Predictive Analytics Work?

How does a predictive model generate a score? That depends on the type of predictive model being employed, and there are quite a few options to choose from. However, two of the most popular types of model are **scorecards** (linear models) and **decision trees** – both of which are relatively easy for non-technical people to understand.

To illustrate these two types of predictive model, let's return to the world of health care, and focus on one specific condition: Heart disease[6]. Heart disease is one of the leading causes of death worldwide. Each year, around 0.1% of the population in western countries (UK, USA, etc.) dies from heart disease, and a significant proportion of the population live with heart conditions that may well kill them sometime down the line. If you can identify people who are highly likely to develop heart disease in the future, and take preventative action to reduce that likelihood, then that will dramatically reduce human suffering and increase life expectancy. The reduction in health care costs will also be considerable.

Imagine that the government has the utopian ideal of screening everyone in the population for heart disease, with the aim of taking preventative action to reduce future incidence of the disease. One way that they could do this is to initiate a programme whereby every man women and child is invited to visit their GP, have relevant investigations and diagnostics tests, and then be given advice on how to minimize their heart disease risk. That's fine in theory, but in practice the cost of such an exercise would be immense, and there would not be enough doctors available to see everyone in a realistic time. The treatment of other life threatening conditions, such as cancer and diabetes, would be likely to suffer due to a lack of resources. In fact, the net result might actually be a reduction in the overall wellbeing of the population, due to an over-emphasis on heart disease at the expense of other conditions.

The blanket approach of screening everyone for heart disease is clearly not realistic. However, a more achievable goal might be to aim to identify say, at least half of those that will develop heart disease in the next 5 years, yet target no more than say, 5% of the population as a whole; i.e. only 1 in 20 people get invited for the full set of tests, but the majority of those likely to get heart disease will be in that 5%. OK – so half of heart disease cases would be missed, but the cost saving is such that it makes the exercise justifiable, and does not threaten resources allocated to the treatment of other conditions.

To achieve this objective we are going to need some way of identifying those most at risk. To do this we are going to build a predictive model that predicts the likelihood of someone developing heart disease in the next few years (a classification model). The aim is to use the model to identify those individuals most at risk, and then contact them to invite them for a check-up and lifestyle review, in order to try and reduce their risk of developing heart disease in the future.

The starting point for predictive analytics is data. Data is the fuel that feeds the predictive analytics process. Trying to do predictive analytics without data is like trying to make a cake without any ingredients or washing your car without water.

To build a model of heart disease, the first task is to gather some historic patient data. For this particular problem, we are going to go back and obtain the medical records from a sample of 500,000 people (chosen at random) who didn't have any sign of heart disease five years ago. This data will include, amongst other things, things like: people's age, gender, their Body Mass Index (BMI)[7], blood pressure readings, previous medical history, how much they exercise, if they smoke, how much alcohol they drink and so on. There may also be other, non-medical information available such as people's income, marital status, number of dependents, type of house they live in and so on, gathered from other sources.

This snapshot of personal data from five years ago is then matched against what happened over the subsequent 5 year **forecast horizon**; i.e. a record is kept of which people went on to develop a heart condition at some time in the next 5 years, and which did not. So at this point we have two parts to the data:

- **Observation data**. This is information about people at the start of the five year period; i.e. their age, blood pressure, smoking habits and so on.

- **Outcome data**. This is a record of their health over the forecast horizon. In particular, this data records if someone developed heart disease or not.

These two types of data, when combined, form the **development sample** that is going to be used to produce the model. Let's assume that of the 500,000 cases in the development sample, 30,000 (6%) went on to develop heart disease and the other 470,000 (94%) did not. Note that having data about people who didn't get heart disease is just as important as having data about those that did. This is because the predictive analytics process works by identifying differences between the two event types. A common mistake with data analysis is just to record data about the event of interest, and to forget about the "non-events." Without both event and non-event information it is very difficult to come to any meaningful conclusions using predictive analytics (or any other data analysis method).

The next stage of the process is where the complex mathematics comes into play. Various mathematical procedures (**Algorithms**) are applied to generate a predictive model based on what the algorithms can infer from the data in the development sample. In particular, the algorithms seek to find relationships that correlate with events or non-events, and it is these relationships that are captured by the predictive model that results.

These days, there are lots of computer packages that will apply the relevant mathematics in order to generate a model. As a rule, you don't need to be a theorist or have a higher degree in mathematics or statistics to be able to generate a predictive model – the software will do it all for you.

Having said this, having some familiarity with the relevant mathematical techniques is helpful. This is because it enables you to understand the diagnostics that the software produces and to identify if there have been any issues with the model creation process. Also, there are often several parameters that need to be set within the software. An experienced data scientist (that's one of the job titles given to people who build predictive models these days)[8] will know how to tweak these parameters to generate a model that is very predictive, and which also meets any business constraints that have been imposed by the organization that commissioned it.

Often the model building process is iterative. Many test models are constructed using different algorithms before a final model is arrived at. Therefore, the analytics process needs someone who knows what they are doing to guide it so that the best overall model is arrived at.

Let's assume that the data scientist starts by considering a **scorecard** type model. After using an appropriate software tool to apply the relevant algorithm to the development sample[9], the software generates the predictive model shown in Figure 2:

Figure 2. A scorecard for predicting heart disease.

Starting score (constant)	350			
Age (years)		**Gross annual income ($)**		
<23	-57	< $22,000		11
23 - 32	-26	$22,001 - $38,000		9
33 - 41	0	$38,001 - $60,000		6
42 - 48	7	$60,001 - $94,000		0
49 - 57	15	$94,001 - $144,000		-5
58 - 64	24	>$144,000		-6
65 - 71	31			
>71	65	**Smoker ?**		
		Yes		37
BMI (weight in kg / {height in metres}^{2})		No		0
<19	2			
19 - 26	0	**Diabetic ?**		
27 - 29	8	Yes		21
30 - 32	14	No		0
>32	29			
		Cholesterol level (mg per decilitre of blood)		
Gender		Low (< 160 mg)		-2
Male	2	Normal (160 - 200 mg)		0
Female	-4	High (201 - 240 mg)		19
		Very high (>240 mg)		32
Alcohol consumption (units/week)				
0	4	**Blood pressure**		
1 - 12	0	Low (below 90/60)		3
13 - 24	5	Average (between 90/60 ar		0
25 - 48	10	High (above 140/90)		36
>48	22			

Using the scorecard in Figure 2, a score for someone is calculated as follows. Everyone starts with the "starting score" of 350. All of the relevant points that apply to that individual are then added or subtracted from the score. For a 45 year old female with the following characteristics:

- A BMI of 28.
- Drinks an average of 6 units of alcohol a week.
- An honours degree graduate.
- An income of $50,000 a year.
- Smokes.
- Is not diabetic.
- Normal cholesterol levels.
- Low blood pressure.

The starting score is 350. Seven points are added due to her age, which brings the score to 357. Eight points are then added based on her BMI, four points subtracted for her gender and no points added (or subtracted) based on her alcohol consumption, and so on. After adding/subtracting all of the relevant points, the final score is 404.

Looking at the scorecard in Figure 2, it's easy to see why scorecards are so attractive, and why they are so widely used across many industry sectors. One reason is that you don't need any technical ability to see which data items contribute to the score someone receives. It's also easy to gauge the relative importance of each data item. For example, age contributes more points to the final score than anything else. Gender on the other hand, only makes a small contribution to the overall score. It's also the case that most data items in the model, such as smoking, alcohol consumption and blood pressure fit with what is generally known from medical studies; i.e. the relationships captured by the model look sensible and conforms with what is already known about risk factors for heart disease.

The fact that the model conforms with what experts already know is useful for getting people to trust the model and be comfortable using it as a diagnostic tool in their day–to-day work. If the model gave negative points for smoking and diabetes, and positive points for normal blood pressure and being young, then that is counter to what every doctor knows. Consequently, people would not have much confidence that the model was correctly predicting the condition, even if the model's predictions were correct.

This appeal to common sense is important, particularly when models are being deployed in an area for the first time. People are often suspicious of new approaches, such as predictive analytics, and may instinctively distrust something that removes the human element from the decision making process. The more that can be done to reassure people that decisions based on the model scores are the right ones, then the easier it will be to overcome any resistance to predictive analytics that is encountered.

The one item in the scorecard that is perhaps slightly unexpected is the impact of someone's income. What the model is saying is that if you have a low income then you are more likely to develop heart disease in the future. If you give this some thought, then it does make sense. If someone is on a low income they may not be able to afford gym membership (less exercise), and they won't spend as much of their income on good quality food.

This ability to pick out new data items that are predictive of something, that an expert might not have considered important before, is one of the big strengths of predictive analytics. This is particularly true as we move further into the world of "Big Data" where there can be tens of thousands of data items available, any one of which could feature in a predictive model – far more than could ever be analyzed by hand.

Predictive analytics is an automated way of sifting all those data items to find the handful that correlate with the behavior being predicted. Having said this, it's important to note that in the vast majority of cases, across many application arears, predictive analytics tends to pick out similar data items to what a human expert would use when making decisions. New, strange or counterintuitive predictive relationships tend to be the exception rather than the rule.

Another thing that gives predictive analytics an edge over human decision makers is that the scores allocated to each data item are optimal, based on the data in the development sample; i.e. the scores assigned to each data item in the model are the best they can be, resulting in the most accurate predictions possible.

Predictive Analytics is not the only way to create scorecard type models. For example, expert opinion can be applied. A group of experts gets together and collectively decide which factors are important and what points should be assigned to those factors. Predictive models constructed in this way often work surprisingly well, but tend to be inferior to models constructed using algorithms to determine the scores from a suitable development sample.

Another interesting feature of the scorecard in Figure 2 is that it only contains 9 data items – yet that's enough to make pretty good predictions, and this is often the case. Very few predictive models need more than a few dozen data items to be able to generate very good predictions indeed. Even if there are many tens of thousands of bits of data available, the vast majority of those data items add little or nothing to the accuracy of predictions. This is a very useful feature of predictive analytics because it means that although a huge amount of data analysis may have been required in order to create a model, far less resource is required when it comes to putting that model to use; i.e. to implement a predictive model you only require the data items that feature in the model. No other data is required.

The scorecard model in Figure 2 predicts the likelihood of someone getting heart disease in the next 5 years. But how do the individual scores generated by the model translate into probabilities? One way to establish the relationship between score and probability is to produce a "score distribution" table as shown in Figure 3.

Figure 3. A score distribution table.

Score range		Number of people	% of population	Number with heart disease after 5 yrs.	% with heart disease after 5 yrs.
From	To				
0	300	55,950	11.19%	40	0.07%
301	320	56,606	11.32%	68	0.12%
321	340	59,700	11.94%	129	0.22%
341	360	58,706	11.74%	216	0.37%
361	380	64,429	12.89%	403	0.63%
381	400	52,749	10.55%	575	1.09%
401	420	34,089	6.82%	600	1.76%
421	440	21,107	4.22%	632	2.99%
441	460	17,269	3.45%	878	5.09%
461	480	23,364	4.67%	2,020	8.65%
481	500	17,477	3.50%	2,553	14.61%
501	520	13,554	2.71%	3,366	24.84%
521	540	7,103	1.42%	3,463	48.76%
541	560	8,260	1.65%	6,587	79.74%
561	999	9,637	1.93%	8,469	87.88%
Total		500,000		30,000	6.0%

To produce Figure 3, a completely new sample of data (a validation sample) was collected for another 500,000 people (30,000 of which went on to develop heart disease over the next 5 years). The **validation sample** is completely independent of the sample used to construct the model. It therefore gives a representative view of how the model will perform when it is applied to new people, whose details were not used to construct the model.[10]

The leftmost column is the score range, showing the range of scores being reported upon in each row. The first row contains details of everyone scoring 300 or less, the second row those scoring between 301 and 320, and so on. Ideally, there would be a separate row for each individual score, but because there are literally hundreds of different scores that can be generated by the model, the scores in this example have been grouped in to 20 point ranges for convenience[11].

The other columns in Figure 3 provide information about the individuals in each score range. For instance, 56,606 cases scored between 301 and 320, representing 11.32% of the cases in the validation sample. Of these, 68 went on to develop heart disease. The rightmost column shows the percentage of people in each score range that developed heart disease. This is, in effect, the prediction made by the model. For those in the 301 − 320 score range, the model prediction is 0.12% To put it another way, anyone whose score is between 301 and 320 has about a 1 in 833 chance of developing heart disease (1/0.0012).

To evaluate the risk of a person getting heart disease in the future, all that one needs to do is:

- Calculate their score using the scorecard in Figure 2.
- Find the row into which their score falls in Figure 3.
- Look across to the rightmost column of Figure 3 to obtain a prediction.

If we return to the case of the 45 year old women who scored 404, she falls in the 401-420 score range. Reading across, the proportion of people who scored between 401 and 420 who went on to develop heart disease was 1.76%. i.e. the model predicts that she has a 1.76% (1 in 57)[12] chance of developing heart disease in the next five years.

If you have the information to hand, then why not have a go at calculating your own score and coming up with a prediction for your own risk of developing heart disease?[13]

Knowing what the score means is important, but the next question is: How well does the scorecard model predict heart disease? One way to evaluate the model is to consider the differences in the rate of heart disease between the lowest and highest scoring cases. Only 0.07% of those scoring 300 or less go on to develop heart disease in the next five years. For those scoring 561 or more, 87.88% develop the condition. To put it another way, people with the highest scores are more than 1,000 times more likely to get heart disease than the people with the lowest scores – which is pretty good.

Another way to approach this is to compare the model's performance against a random selection strategy; i.e. if you select people at random for check-ups, then only 6% of those people would go on to get heart disease, whereas the best scoring group (561-999) performs about 15 times better than this (87.88 / 6).

Appendix A provides a more detailed explanation of the most common metrics used by data scientists to evaluate how good predictive models are at predicting behaviour.

6 Using a Predictive Model to Make Decisions

By this point we:

- Have a predictive model (the scorecard in Figure 2).
- Understand what the scores means.
- Know the probability of someone getting heart disease given their score (from the information provided in Figure 3).
- Have a feel for how much better the scorecard is at identifying heart disease sufferers than a random selection policy.
- Know the distribution of the population across the range of possible scores (from the information in Figure 3).

That's all well and good, but none of this information tells us what to do on the basis of the score that someone receives. If the model is going to provide value, then decisions need to be made and those decisions acted upon. If someone receives a score of say 517, are they invited for a check-up or not?

Before going further, let's cast our minds back to the start of the previous chapter, where the following objective was laid out:

- Identify at least half of those who will develop heart disease in the next 5 years, and then invite them to visit their doctor for a more in-depth check-up.

Subject to the following constraint:

- No more than 5% of the population can be invited for a check-up; i.e. there are sufficient resources for 1 in every 20 people to be seen by their doctor.

To answer the question, we need to refer back to the score distribution that was introduced in Figure 3. To save you having to refer back to it, it has been reproduced as Figure 4 below.

Figure 4. Deja vu. A score distribution table (again!)

| Score range | | Number of | % of | Number with | % with heart |
From	To	people	population	heart disease after 5 yrs.	disease after 5 yrs.
0	300	55,950	11.19%	40	0.07%
301	320	56,606	11.32%	68	0.12%
321	340	59,700	11.94%	129	0.22%
341	360	58,706	11.74%	216	0.37%
361	380	64,429	12.89%	403	0.63%
381	400	52,749	10.55%	575	1.09%
401	420	34,089	6.82%	600	1.76%
421	440	21,107	4.22%	632	2.99%
441	460	17,269	3.45%	878	5.09%
461	480	23,364	4.67%	2,020	8.65%
481	500	17,477	3.50%	2,553	14.61%
501	520	13,554	2.71%	3,366	24.84%
521	540	7,103	1.42%	3,463	48.76%
541	560	8,260	1.65%	6,587	79.74%
561	999	9,637	1.93%	8,469	87.88%
Total		500,000		30,000	6.0%

The limiting factor (the constraint) in this problem is doctors' time. At most, 1 in 20 people (5%) can be invited for a check-up. Using the information from the "% of population" column in Figure 4 to do some simple arithmetic, it can be determined that:

- 1.93% of the population scores 561 or more.
- 3.58% of the population scores 541 or more.
- *5.00% of the population scores 521 or more.*
- 7.71% of the population scores 501 or more.
- And so on...

Therefore, the **cut-off strategy** (decision rule) to apply is:

- Invite anyone scoring 521 or more for a check-up and lifestyle review with their doctor.

The final step is to evaluate the impact of the decision rule. How good will the scorecard based decision making process be? Will the model be able to identify at least 50% of heart disease sufferers within the group scoring 521 or more?

Looking at the second rightmost column in Figure 4, there are 18,519 (3,463 + 6,587 + 8,469) cases scoring 521 or more. That's 62% of the total 30,000 cases of heart disease. That's pretty good isn't it? By selecting just the 5% of the population scoring 521 or more, 62% of all heart disease cases can be identified. The objective (to identify at least 50%) has been met.

These figures are based on the 500,000 people in the validation sample. Given that this is a large independent sample, it's a reasonably safe assumption that the results are representative of what would be observed if the model was applied to the country's entire population of many tens of millions[14].

As I've already mentioned, predictive models aren't perfect. Some of those scoring 521 or more won't get heart disease. Using the data in the score distribution table again, it's relatively easy to work out how often the model gets it right for this particular decision rule, and how often it gets it wrong. There are 25,000 cases scoring 521 or more. Of these 18,519 get heart disease. Therefore, the overall hit rate is 74% (100 * 18,519/25,000), which means that 26% of those invited for a check-up don't really need one. Not perfect, but far far better than selecting people at random from the population. With only 6% of the population expected to develop heart disease in the next five years, a random invitation strategy would result in 94% (100% − 6%) of the check-ups being wasted on people who were not going to get heart disease in the first place.

Score distribution tables, such as those in Figure 4, underpin all of the reporting and performance metrics that support the evaluation and use of predictive models. In real world applications they tend to be much more granular (have more rows) and contain additional columns containing information such as cumulative ascending/descending numbers and percentages to aid with calculations.

Some people (particularly old hands like me who began doing predictive analytics before tools like Excel were common) prefer to work directly from score distribution tables like the one in Figure 4. However, these days there are many superb visualization tools that can be used to present the results from the score distribution table in more intuitive and user friendly ways. The best tools are also interactive. They allow you to experiment with different models, constraints and cut-off strategies to find the best decision rules for your particular problem.

Two of the most popular ways of providing a graphical representation of a score distribution table are **Lift charts** and **Gain charts**. These are described in Appendix A.

7 That's Scorecards, but What About Decision Trees?

Decision trees are another popular type of predictive model. Like scorecards, they are also very easy to understand and use.

To demonstrate what decision trees look like and how they work, let's continue with the problem of heart disease; i.e. the objective is to come up with a way to identify at least half of those who will go on to develop heart disease, but to invite no more than 1 in 20 (5%) of the population to come for a check-up with their doctor.

To build a decision tree model, the 500,000 cases that were used to build the scorecard are used again, but this time a different algorithm is used to derive a model from the data. Figure 5 shows the structure of the resulting decision tree model.

To calculate a score for someone using the decision tree, one starts at the top of the tree at the first node (Entire population). One then moves down the tree. At each branching point the node is chosen that fits that person's individual characteristics. In Figure 5, the first branching is based on age. If a person is less than 52 years old, then the left hand side of the tree is followed. If they are aged 52 years or more, then the right hand branch is followed. The process is repeated at each decision point until there are no further decisions to be made. The final node (called an end node or leaf node) into which a person falls determines their score.

In Figure 5, there are 13 end nodes (shaded in grey and numbered) and hence 13 scores that someone can receive. Those scoring 1 have the lowest chance of developing heart disease, those scoring 13 the highest.

Figure 5. A decision tree model.

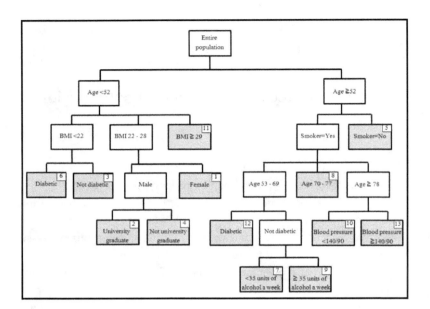

In terms of how the scores generated by the decision tree are used, the process is virtually identical to that for the scorecard. The details of the 500,000 people from the validation sample are run through the decision tree to obtain scores, and a score distribution table is then produced showing how the scores are distributed. Figure 6 shows the score distribution table for the decision tree.

Going through the same process that we followed for the scorecard, the highest scoring 5% of the population is covered by those scoring 12 or 13. Of these, 16,910 subsequently go on to develop heart disease, which is 55% of the total number of cases. Therefore, the targeting strategy for inviting people for a check-up is to invite all those scoring 12 or 13.

Like the scorecard, this strategy also meets the stated objective of inviting no more than 5% of the total population for a check-up, but to have at least half of all those who will go on to develop heart disease within that 5%

Figure 6. Score distribution for the decision tree model.

Node (Score)	Number of people	% of population	Number with heart disease after 5 yrs.	% with heart disease after 5 yrs.
1	98,760	19.75%	109	0.11%
2	104,324	20.86%	177	0.17%
3	32,176	6.44%	93	0.29%
4	78,287	15.66%	385	0.49%
5	19,998	4.00%	162	0.81%
6	28,675	5.74%	460	1.60%
7	48,748	9.75%	1,581	3.24%
8	22,801	4.56%	1,491	6.54%
9	18,884	3.78%	2,452	12.98%
10	15,034	3.01%	3,419	22.74%
11	7,313	1.46%	2,763	37.78%
12	18,901	3.78%	11,889	62.90%
13	6,099	1.22%	5,021	82.32%
Total	**500,000**		**30,000**	**6.0%**

OK. We now have two models. The question that will now be on many peoples' lips is: which is the best model? Is it the scorecard or the decision tree? When people ask this question, what they usually want to know is: which model generates the most accurate predictions?

In this particular example, both models provided sufficient predictive accuracy to meet the stated objective, but the scorecard is better. This is because if you use the scorecard to decide which 5% of the population to invite for a check-up (those scoring 521 or more), you would expect to invite 62% of those who go on to develop heart disease. The decision tree on the other hand only identifies 55% of them (those scoring 12 or 13).

At this point it's worth making some observations about the similarities and differences between the decision tree model and the scorecard model. Some important things to note are:

- The decision tree and scorecard use similar, but not identical data items to make predictions. The scorecard includes annual income, but the decision tree does not. Likewise "Graduate" features in the decision tree model but not the scorecard.

- The branch conditions in the decision tree don't always align with the score ranges in the scorecard. In the scorecard, age breaks occur at 49 and 57, but in the decision tree the key age split is at 52 years old (with additional age splits further down the tree).

- The decision tree generates 13 possible scores, whereas there are hundreds of scores that can be generated by the scorecard; i.e. the scorecard generates a much more granular range of scores than the decisions tree.

The fact that the scorecard and decision tree models have differences in the data that they use is a feature of the algorithms used to construct them. There are literally hundreds of different algorithms that can be used to construct many different types of predictive model, and each algorithm has its own logic for selecting which data items are important predictors, and what weight those predictors should be given in the model. Each modelling approach has its strengths and weakness, and is better at predicting some types of cases than others.

What this means in practice is that there no such thing as a best type of model, which should always be used for all types of problem. No one type of predictive model can be said to be universally better than all the others. The scorecard proved to be better (in terms of predictive accuracy) than the decision tree this time, but for a different type of problem, using different data and with different objectives, it may well be the case that a decision tree wins out.

This means is that if you want to ensure that you get the very best model for your particular problem (as measured in terms of predictive accuracy), you have to build different models, compare them against each other, and then decide which one is the most appropriate.

Having said this, in practical real world situations, most types of model yield very similar levels of predictive performance for many types of problem[15]. There may be theoretical arguments as to why one type of model is better than another, or why Algorithm A is superior to Algorithm B, but in practice they are all much of a muchness. Therefore, there is a good deal of latitude that can be applied when selecting which type of model to choose.

This is another great feature of predictive analytics. This is because it means that other factors, in addition to predictive accuracy, can come into play when deciding which model is best for a given problem. In particular, in some problem domains, having a model that is easily explicable and which is aligned to a common sense view as to how decisions should be made is vital. This is sometimes far more important than having a model that is theoretically more appropriate or marginally more accurate, but which is less well understood by business users.

8 Putting Predictive Analytics to Work

Some organizations have been using predictive analytics for decades. This is particularly true in the financial services industry, and in the marketing departments of large consumer facing organizations such as supermarkets. Consequently, these organizations have well-established IT infrastructures, systems and processes for building and implementing predictive models. They do it day in, day out – it's just business as usual.

For organizations that are new to predictive analytics, building a predictive model for the first time, and then operationalizing it, can be a difficult task. Sometimes it can take several months before the required data is ready and the predictive analytics process can be applied. However, gathering the right data and then building a predictive model are often the easiest parts of a predictive analytics project. This is because, at the end of the day, a predictive model is nothing more than a set of equations captured in a spreadsheet, a word document or other software. The model needs to be operationalized if it's going to be of use.

The main challenge, particularly for organizations that have not used predictive analytics before, is to accept the use of automated decision making. They need to put in place the infrastructure to allow predictive models to become a key part of the organization's operational decision making capability, and to be comfortable with the decisions that are made on the basis of the model's predictions. This includes establishing governance procedures to ensure that model based decisions are acted upon as intended, and that these decisions are not ignored or over-ridden by human decisions makers, except in specific pre-agreed situations.

Perhaps the biggest mistake an organization can make is to assume that successful predictive analytics is: "All about the model" when they should be thinking about things from the perspective of: "It's all about the business."

Predictive analytics may be something that can add value to what an organization does, but then again it may not. A useful analogy is building a car engine. The engineers can spend a lot of time building a very powerful and efficient engine. However, that engine isn't going to provide any benefit unless someone has thought about the design of the car body, the engine mounting and so on, into which the engine will be placed. Without the rest of the car the engine is useless. The same applies to predictive analytics. Unless there is a business process to slot the model into, the model won't be of much use.

If an organization is going to successfully integrate predictive analytics into its business processes, then there are five core areas that need to be considered, in the following order:

1. **Problem.** What is predictive analytics going to be used for? There needs to be a clear problem that predictive analytics can help with.

2. **Culture.** Can the business be persuaded to accept predictive analytics? Will they allow it to drive automated decision making? From a managerial perspective, are resources (i.e. people and money) available to enable predictive analytics to be integrated into the relevant business process?

3. **Model Implementation.** What system or process will be used to put the model into practice? How will scores be calculated? How will decisions made on the basis of those scores be acted upon by the relevant business function?

4. **Development Data**. Does sufficient data exist to enable predictive models to be constructed?

5. **Analytics**. Does the organization have the software tools and expertise required to analyse data and build predictive models?

At first sight, the ordering of this list may seem somewhat counterintuitive. Why, for example, is model implementation listed before the analytics? Surely one builds a model first, and then thinks about implementing it?

Predictive analytics is good for a lot of things, but it's not always the case that a predictive model is what you need. Likewise, just because it's technically possible to predict something, it doesn't mean that you should, or that the predictions will provide value. Therefore, one needs to begin with problem specification and a plan about how to address it. Thought needs to be given to how you are going to use a predictive model within an organization before you develop it and so on.

If predictive analytics is going to be the answer, then the two critical items that need to be established before anything else is done are:

- What is the uncertain event/value/thing that you want to predict? This needs to be something very clear and explicit. It needs to be easily measurable, and can be represented as a simple "yes/no" for classification problems, or as a numeric value for regression problems.

- What decisions will be taken about how to treat people, on the basis of the predictions made by the model?

There is no point developing a predictive model to predict events that are certainly going to occur. Likewise, if people will continue to be treated in the same way, regardless of the score that they receive, then what use is the model? For example, if existing customers are always going to be offered the same level of discount off their next purchase, then there is no point building a predictive model to identify repeat shoppers. A repeat shopper model will only be useful if a differential incentive strategy is offered, based on the scores generated by the model. For example, not offering a discount to those the model predicts almost certainly will buy again (high scores), and offering large discounts to those at the other end of the scale (low scores), to encourage them to shop again at the store.

Identifying the right problem is critical. One limitation of predictive analytics is that it is very specific. If we stick with the repeat shopper problem, is the objective to predict repeat shoppers, or to identify profitable customers? The answer probably depends on what market you are in, but in some markets, small frequent repeat buyers generate less profit than those making less frequent, but larger purchases. In these markets, if efforts are focused on encouraging repeat purchases per se, then the numbers of transactions may increase, but overall profitability declines – not what was intended! Likewise, a model built to predict heart disease will probably not be very good predicting Dementia and vice versa.

The second consideration when building predictive models is organizational culture, and the appetite for change within business areas that will be impacted by the use of models. Existing working practices and resistance to new ways of working are often a barrier to the introduction of predictive analytics. This is particularly true when staff are expected to behave differently on the basis of what the model tells them; i.e. predictive analytics is going to change the way people do their jobs; and in some cases it will result in job losses and/or a devaluation of their skills.

As a rule, experts in a field don't tend to trust predictive models to be as good as they are at predicting the outcomes from a given situation. What this means is that an expert will often override decisions made on the basis of a predictive model, if they are given the opportunity to do so - in effect negating any benefits that the model would have delivered.

Whether overriding is going to be a problem or not, often rests on whether the predictive model is implemented in an active or passive way:

- **Active Models.** The predictions (scores) generated by a model are acted upon automatically. No human involvement is required for actions to be carried out.

- **Passive Models.** The model scores are used to generate cases that are passed on to people, who then decide how to deal with them; i.e. nothing happens until someone does something with the cases generated by the analytics process.

An example of an active model is in debt collection. Predictive models are widely used to prioritize debtors on the basis of which ones are most likely to repay what they owe. The prioritized lists are loaded into a dialer which then automatically calls people in list order.

When contact is made with a debtor, the call is transferred to a human debt collector who tries to persuade the debtor to repay what they owe. The debt collectors themselves aren't concerned with the order in which cases are presented to them. They simply process each case that is referred to them. Consequently, once the model has been implemented, then no further human input is required to decide on the ordering of the call list maintained by the dialer.

An example of a passive model on the other hand, is one that has been designed to select the best job applicants for a particular role. The model may be very good at picking out the most promising prospects, but a human interviewer is still required to make the final decision about a job offer. If the interviewer takes a dislike to a candidate for whatever reason, then they won't offer the candidate the job, regardless of how good they would actually be at doing it.

Passive models are the most problematic. This is because in many organizations, those at the front line have the ability to change or alter decisions that were made centrally. In the recruitment example, the power of the model is increasingly diminished the more the interviewers decide to override model based decision with their own. Likewise, human assessors often display bias (consciously or unconsciously) that disadvantages good candidates based on some unfound prejudice or stereotype, resulting in many good candidates having their job applications turned down.

Another example that I came across was in tax collection. A central function was responsible for identifying potentially fraudulent tax returns, and these cases were then passed on to locally based tax inspectors to carryout detailed investigations. The tax inspectors had the power to reject cases that they felt weren't suitable, or which were unlikely to yield much additional tax.

When the central function implemented a predictive model to identify cases that were highly likely to be fraudulent, the number of cases rejected by the tax inspectors rose dramatically. This wasn't because the cases generated by the model weren't fraudulent. It was because the model was too good at identifying fraudulent activity due to very subtle signs in the data.

When a case arrived on a tax inspector's desk, the inspector was unable to establish exactly what was fishy about it. Therefore they did not know how to go about beginning an investigation, and consequently they rejected it. Likewise, the model often selected cases that were very complex, or where it would be very difficult to collect the unpaid tax even though fraud had clearly occurred.[16] These types of cases also had a tendency to be rejected.

Active models are much easier to implement successfully than passive models. This is because people don't have the opportunity to override model based decisions. For example, once a decision has been made to post a customer a discount voucher, the process of dispatching the voucher, with a covering letter, is automatic. No one is second guessing the system and giving vouchers to customer that they believe don't want them or won't use them. This is one reason why predictive analytics has been such as success for things like target marketing, credit granting and insurance pricing, yet is less well utilized in areas such as health care, human resources, policing and education.

The third item in the checklist, after problem definition and culture is implementation. As discussed earlier, predictive analytics is all about making faster, better and cheaper decisions. Predictive models can be implemented manually in a spread sheet and scores can even be calculated using a pen and paper, but in most cases predictive models are embedded within an automated decision making system. The system uses the model to make predictions about how people will behave, and then takes decisions about how to treat people based on those predictions; e.g. the decision to grant a loan if the score is high enough.

By automating the decision making process, individually tailored strategies for dealing with millions of people can enacted in just a few seconds. What this means in practice is that organizations can update their predictions about people on a very frequent basis: monthly, daily, or even in real time, whenever a new piece of information about an individual is obtained.

Far more predictive models get developed than are ever implemented operationally. I've lost count of the number of organizations I've worked with where everyone gets really excited about the model building process, but then neglects to think about how they are going to put the model to use once they have it. Unless the infrastructure for predictive analytics is already well established, then the implementation of a predictive model is often a more lengthy and time consuming process than getting the model built in the first place. Therefore, this needs to be considered, budget approved and planning begun, long before the data scientists are let loose to start gathering data and building models[17].

Generally, there are two ways that organizations implement models. The first approach is to treat implementation as an IT project. A programmer is employed to "code up" the model within an organization's IT system, so that the required scores are calculated when and where they are needed. This is a common approach, but it's amazing how often models are incorrectly coded due to simple errors – such as giving someone 100 points instead of 10, or plus 15 points instead of minus 15 points. There are also prioritization issues to contend with, and it's not unusual for model implementation to take months or even years, due to other tasks taking priority. It's also the case that following implementation, trying to get changes to a model or the associated cut-off rules is a nightmare, because every change has to go back into the IT work queue for prioritization.

The second approach to model implementation is via specialist software that provides an interface between the software used to build the model and the operational environment where the model is deployed. When the model is complete the model builder simply hits the "upload" button in the software, which then deploys the model (and associated cut-off rules) to the operational environment.

The main benefit of this approach is that in theory, models can be implemented almost as soon as they are built, and it is the Data Scientist who controls the implementation of the model and associated cut-off (decision) rules. Little or no IT input is required, which avoids lengthy delays that might otherwise arise if model implementation were to be placed in the IT work queue.

The penultimate consideration, before the analytics process can begin, is data. Data is the primary ingredient in the analytics process. It's essential. Without data, and the right type of data, useful predictive models cannot be constructed or deployed. Therefore, before any thought is given to running algorithms to build a predictive model, due consideration needs to be given to the data that is going to be used. In particular:

- **Development sample data.** As discussed in Section 5, a reasonably sized sample of data is required which includes both historic observation data and more recent outcome data.

- **Operational availability.** Any data that features in the resulting model must be available when the model comes to be implemented.

- **Operational stability.** If the relationships in data change, then a model based on that data will lose some of its predictive ability. Therefore, a new model will be required.

It's important to remember that the development sample used to build a predictive model is historic. It comes from the past, but the predictive model that is constructed from it is going to be deployed in the future. In the months or years since the development sample data was recorded, there may have been significant changes to the way the organization gathers and stores data. If certain data items are not going to be available going forward, then those data items should not be used to build the model. This is because it will not be possible to put the model into production. The data needed by the model simply won't be available.

It may be that in the past net income was obtained from customers and this is what is contained in the development sample data. However, because net income is sometimes difficult for customers to remember, the marketing department decided that it would be more customer friendly to switch to capturing gross income instead. Therefore, if a predictive model was built using net income, it would not be possible to implement the model correctly because net income would no longer be available following the change to the way income is captured[18].

Once the problem has been specified, and cultural, implementation and data issues have been considered, then one can start to think about the analytical process of building the model. This is where the specialist skills of a data scientist come into their own.

When it comes to the technical aspects of building a predictive model, a data scientist needs to consider a range of issues. Generating the most predictive model possible is obviously one concern, but the complexity, explicability and transparency of the resulting solution also need to be considered in light of organizational and regulatory requirements.

In banking, for example, the predictive models used to generate estimates of the capital that banks must hold are subject to extreme scrutiny by banking regulators. The model builder must fully describe the analytical process that was applied to construct the model, explain exactly how the model generates its predictions, and then highlight any material weaknesses that the model may have.

"Black box" solutions that simply spit out very accurate, but inexplicable predictions will not pass muster. Likewise, in areas such as tax collection, medical diagnosis and criminal investigation, subject matter experts often favor models that they can understand. However, if we shift the emphasis to models that are used in target marketing, or those used to select matches on dating sites, then the user has far less interest in understanding the underlying model logic – predictive accuracy is the overriding consideration. If it works it works, and that's all that matters.

Before choosing which type of model to develop and what algorithm to apply, a data scientist should have consulted with the business. They should have asked the right questions to make sure that they deliver a model that is predictive, conforms to regulatory requirements and takes into account any other issues or constraints that the business has highlighted.

Once the analytical process is complete and a predictive model is available, then it can be transferred to the area where it will be implemented. Assuming model implementation was given due consideration at the right point in the project, then this should be a relatively smooth process because the necessary software and IT should already have been deployed, and the relevant operational staff briefed about how things will change when the model comes on-line.

Implementing an automated decision making process, based on predictive analytics is a great achievement, particularly if it's something new for the organization in question. However, that's not the end of the process. Once a model goes live, the decision making process needs to be the subject of regular review to assess how well the model is predicting, and to ensure that the right cut-offs and decision rules continue to be applied.

Monitoring is required because a model's predictive accuracy tends to decline over time due to changes in the underlying relationships between the data used to construct the model and the outcome being predicted. Monitoring usually involves producing a set of reports showing how accurate the predictions made by the model proved to be. When model accuracy begins to fall, then that indicates that it's time for a new model to be developed.

Fall in predictive accuracy as models age is the primary reason why models need to be redeveloped, but predictive models are also redeveloped for other reasons. Sometimes there are legal or regulatory changes, which mean that certain data items that feature in a model can no longer be used for decision making. Likewise, new data sources become available, holding out the promise that better, more predictive models, can be constructed.

Another reason for carrying out regular monitoring of a model is to assess how the decisions based on the model affect different groups within the population. If the marketing department of a bank wants to target people with a certain geo-demographic profile with a new type of credit card, then it's important for the bank to understand how its credit scoring models, used to decide which credit card applications to accept, treats those types of people. The last thing the bank wants to do is undertake a huge marketing campaign for new customers and then see all those that apply for the new card being declined.

Likewise, if models are involved in making important or life changing decisions about people, then it is prudent to monitor the model to ensure that any biases in the model are acceptable, and if they are not, to correct for that bias. If an HR department is using a model to screen job applicants, then if the model is found to be rejecting a high proportion of people from ethnic minorities or women, then that will need to be investigated and remedial action taken if necessary.

9 The Relationship Between Big Data and Predictive Analytics

Since about 2010, "Big Data" has become the ubiquitous term used to describe all the data that is generated by people from their smart phones, web browsing history, social media and purchasing behaviour, together with any other information that organizations hold about them[19].

Why is Big Data different to any other type of data? In one sense, there isn't a difference; it's all just zeros and ones at the end of the day. However, the term "Big Data" tends to be applied to large collections of different types of data which are often volatile and changeable, and where one would struggle to analyze it using traditional computer hardware and software.

It's also the case that Big Data often incorporates certain types of data that were not widely used for customer analysis until relatively recently. In particular, Big Data includes:

- **Text.** What people write and say can be analysed to identify what they are talking about and the sentiments being expressed. If a product is being discussed in a positive or negative context, this is likely to be predictive of whether someone goes on to buy that product.

- **Images.** This covers photos and video, as well as medical imaging. One application of predictive analytics is to use features identified in scans and x-rays to predict the likelihood that someone has a specific disease.

- **(Social) network data.** This is information about people's connections and who they know. Network data includes the number and type of connections that people have, as well as data about connected individuals. If all your friends are sci-fi geeks, that's probably a good indication that you might be one too.

- **Geospatial.** Information about peoples' location and movements, provided by smart phones and other mobile devices.

- **Biometrics.** Data about blood pressure, heart rate and so on, collected from fit bands, smart watches and so on.

- **Product (machine) generated.** Everyday devices from washing machines to coffee makers are being designed to share information between themselves and over the internet. These days your heating, kettle and washing machine can be programmed to turn themselves on when your smart phone indicates you are on your way home from work. The "Internet of Things" (IoT) concept is still developing, but will eventually provide lots of data that can be used to infer people's behaviour using predictive analytics.

In the "good old days" back in the 1990s, smart devices didn't exist. Few people even had a cell phone back then, and the internet was still in its infancy. Very little electronic data about people or their activities existed. What there was was usually limited to a few geo-demographics such as address, age, income, gender and so on. This may then have been supplemented by data supplied from a direct marketing company or a credit reference agency if financial services products were involved (e.g. arrears status on loans and credit cards). Supermarkets had no idea what individual customers bought each week, insurance companies didn't know how people drove, and health services held most of their patient records in paper files.

Life for a data scientist back then was pretty straightforward[20] because all of this (very limited) electronic data was usually held in a nice neat format of rows and columns (like one would find in a spreadsheet). The data was also relatively static, usually only being updated very infrequently – typically at month or year end.

In today's world of Big Data, data is being updated much more frequently, often in real time. In addition, a lot more of it is "free form" unstructured data such as speech, e-mail, tweets, blogs and so on. Another factor is that much of this data is often generated independently of the organization that wants to use it. This is problematic, because if data is captured or generated by an organization itself, then they can control how that data is formatted, and put checks and controls in place to ensure that the data is accurate and complete. However, if data is being generated from external sources, then there are no guarantees that the data is correct.

Externally sourced data is often "Messy." It requires a significant amount of work to tidy it up and to get it in to a useable format. In addition, there may be concerns over the stability and on-going availability of that data, which presents a business risk if it becomes part of an organization's core decision making capability.

What this means is that traditional computer architectures (Hardware and software) that organizations use for things like processing sales transactions, maintaining customer account records, billing and debt collection, are not well suited to storing and analyzing all of the new and different types of data that are now available. Consequently, over the last few years a whole host of new and interesting hardware and software solutions have been developed to deal with these new types of data.

In particular, modern Big Data computer systems are good at:

- **Storing massive amounts of data.** Traditional databases are limited in the amount of data that they can hold at reasonable cost. New ways of storing data has allowed an almost limitless expansion in cheap storage capacity.

- **Data cleaning and formatting**. Diverse and messy data needs to be transformed into a standard format before it can be used for predictive analytics, management reporting or other data related tasks[21].

- **Processing data very quickly**. Big data is not just about there being more data. It needs to be processed and analysed quickly to be of greatest use.

The issue with traditional computer systems wasn't that there was any theoretically barrier to them undertaking the processing required to utilize Big Data, but in practice they were too slow, too cumbersome and too expensive to do so.

New data storage and processing paradigms such as **Hadoop/MapReduce** have enabled processing tasks that would have taken weeks or months to be undertaken in just a few hours, and at a fraction of the cost of more traditional data processing approaches. The way that Hadoop does this is to allow data and data processing to be spread across networks of cheap desktop PCs. In theory, tens of thousands of PCs can connected together to deliver massive computational capabilities that are comparable to the largest supercomputers in existence.

Data (whether "Big" or "Small") has no intrinsic value in itself. A big mistake that an organization can make is to think that if they invest in a mass storage system, such as Hadoop, and collect every scrap of data they can about people, then that's going to add value. The data has to be worked into something useful if it's going to be of benefit. Predictive Analytics is the key tool that does that – applying algorithms to all that data and producing predictive models that can tell you something about people's future behaviour, based on what has happened before in the past.

A good way to think about the relationship between Big Data and Predictive Analytics is that the data is the raw material that feeds the analytical process. The tangible benefit to a business is derived from the predictive model that comes out at the end of the process, not the data used to construct it.

Predictive analytics and Big Data are therefore often talked about in the same breath, but it's not a symmetrical relationship. You need Predictive Analytics to get the best out of Big Data, but you don't need Big Data to be able use predictive analytics effectively. If you have a just few items of information about a few hundred people then that's enough to begin building predictive models and making useful predictions.

The more and better data that you have, then the better at making predictions your models will be, but having gigabytes or terabytes of data is not a prerequisite for building useful models.

10 Ethical Considerations

The use of predictive models raises some interesting ethical questions. This is especially true when they form part of an automated system that is making decisions about millions of people without any human involvement.

As predictive analytics becomes ever more widely used across many different aspects of our lives, then what we are saying is that in effect, we are no longer in control. Those once in positions of authority, whether it's a bank manger deciding who to lend to, or a doctor deciding who to treat, have ceded control to the computers.

Is this a problem? If one could say categorically that the result would always be better outcomes for individuals then that would be acceptable to many people. However, it's important to appreciate that in many, and possibly most situations, organizations are using predictive analytics for their own benefit to further their own objectives (i.e. maximize profit). Whether or not the resulting outcomes benefit the people who are the subject of those decisions is not their primary concern.

The implication is that as a society we need to be comfortable with the way that predictive models are being developed and deployed, and that this aligns with our sense of what is right and proper. Therefore, appropriate checks and balances need to be in place to prevent misuse of predictive analytics.

The problem is that what constitutes "ethical use" is not always clear cut. There are a range of views and opinions as to what is or is not ethical when it comes to data and analytics. Therefore, what checks and controls are required is somewhat debatable.

One argument is that if a predictive model generates superior predictions, resulting in better, faster and cheaper decision making than that made by human experts, then that's obviously the right thing to do. However, it's important to realize that the ends do not always justify the means. How one gets to a decision, and what is considered to be acceptable by wider society is also important.

Let's start by thinking about the data that is used to make predictions about peoples' behaviour. Do you think it is acceptable to use information about someone's gender, age, religion, marital status, sexual orientation or race when deciding how someone is dealt with? i.e. should this type of data be allowed to feature in a predictive model?

To be fair, this is something of a trick question. The answer will be influenced by the type of decision being made. If we are talking about diagnosis or treatment of a medical condition, then most people would probably not be too concerned with any of this type of data being used if it leads to better outcomes for individuals. The fact that age and gender, for example, were predictive in the heart disease model (Figure 2) is not an issue. However, if we are talking about deciding who to hire or fire on the basis of things like gender or marital status, or charging people more for products or services because of their religion, then things are less clear.

From a purely statistical perspective, things like marital status, gender and age may indeed be correlated with things such as how well people perform in their jobs (And hence who to hire or fire). However, from a societal perspective, allowing a predictive model to drive decisions based on this type of data is ethically questionable and is illegal in many jurisdictions.

A very simple and simplistic solution to problems like this is to make sure that certain data items are prevented from featuring in some types of predictive model to ensure legal compliance. The algorithm that generates a predictive model is directed to exclude data such as gender, race and marital status from the predictive analytics process. That's fine, but just because a predictive model does not use certain data items directly, doesn't mean that the model does not display unacceptable bias.

A great example of this is gender discrimination in insurance. It's a well-established fact that women present a lower risk than men for many types of insurance. However, in all countries that are members of the EU it is illegal to set insurance premiums on the basis of gender. Therefore insurers don't use gender in the claims prediction models that they use to set premiums. However, there are other variables that often act as a proxy for gender. Income, for example, is one such type of data. Why? Because there is gender bias in income distributions. Women, on average, earn less than men, even when they are doing the same job, and even though wage discrimination on the grounds of gender is illegal. Therefore, if a predictive model uses income as a predictor variable, there is an indirect effect which means that women will be treated differently to men. As a consequence, a predictive model may have to be designed to be sub-optimal in terms of predictive ability. This is to ensure that, all other things being equal, it generates the same predictions for men and women with the same characteristics.

Predictive models should conform with legal and regulatory requirements – such as not displaying gender bias. However, that's not the end of the story. A very easy mistake to make is to think that if it's legal then it must also be ethical. Sure, there is some relationship between what's ethical and what's legal, but they are not the same thing. Laws often seek to define behaviour which society deems unacceptable (i.e. unethical), but at best, laws are generalizations of ethical behaviour, and are usually retrospective in nature.

Laws tend to address problems that occurred in the past; they don't usually consider new situations before they arise. Consequently, there are always situations that are not covered by specific laws and there are always loopholes which exist to allow the unscrupulous to get what they want. This is what people mean when they talk about the letter of the law as opposed to the spirit of the law.

OK - so an organization can be acting legally but not ethically, but why should a business that is concerned with maximizing the bottom line be concerned by that? One reason is pure self-interest. There is a lot of evidence that if one is thinking about the long term, then adopting an ethical code of behaviour delivers a real bottom line benefit.[22]

Another reason for thinking about ethical issues within the context of predictive analytics, and the data that predictive models use, is the risk of reputational damage. If the public decide that they don't like the way you operate, think that you treat people in an underhand way, or unfairly discriminate against certain groups, then those sentiments can devalue a brand immensely. Simply arguing that your predictive model is statistically valid isn't enough. If it comes to light that a model puts war veterans, and children at the back of the queue for medical treatment (even though being a war veteran or a child are not explicit variables in the model) then you are going to be challenged about that – even if the decision making process that uses the predictive model generates optimal patient outcomes measured across the population as a whole.

Another way to think about this is that ethical considerations should drive a number of constraints within decision making systems, which need to be given appropriate consideration when the system is designed.

What should an organization do to incorporate an ethical perspective into their use of predictive analytics? Unfortunately there is not a clear cut answer to this question. One problem is the subjective nature of ethics. It's very much a personal thing. Two people may hold opposing, but equally valid opinions as to what constitutes acceptable behaviour. Likewise, different legislative regimes approach personal data and how organization can use it in very different ways.

In the USA, the starting point when it comes to personal data (and its use within automated decision making systems) is very much along utilitarian lines. Personal data is there to be harvested and used to maximize organizational goals (e.g. maximize profit or minimize cost). If there is a problem using a specific type of data, or there is unacceptable bias against a specific group, then legislation is enacted to address that particular concern.

This is very different to the rights based approach adopted by countries within the European Union. The foundation stone of EU data protection law is personal ownership of one's data. Data about me is mine – you have no right to hold or use my data unless I give you permission to do so. If I don't want my data to be used for a given purpose, then that's my decision, even if that leads to sub-optimal outcomes.

These two different perspectives are one reason why US based companies such as Google and Facebook, struggle to find common ground with regulators over how personal data can be gathered and used in EU countries.

Another issue is that ethical considerations are often problem and domain specific. What's acceptable in one situation is not acceptable in another. As we've already discussed, most people are probably OK with sensitive personal information, such as their religion and sexual orientation, being used to diagnose a medical condition. However, using these same data items to decide who can or cannot get a mortgage is a far more questionable proposition.

Given the complexity around these issues, it's good practice for the builders of automated decision making systems to undertake an ethical risk assessment as part of the design phase of the project. In assessing the ethical risk associated with an automated decision making system there are three main aspects to consider:

1. **Benefit.** Who is going to gain from the decision being made? The more the decision maker benefits at the expense of the individual, the greater the ethical risk that that decision represents. An employer deciding who to employ, is making a decisions purely for their own benefit. Jobs are not offered on the basis of the benefit they give to the employee.

2. **Data Immutability.** There are some characteristics people are born with. These can't change. If decisions are made on the basis of things such as age and ethnic origin, then that's far more controversial than data that results from people's lifestyle choices, which is more dynamic and changeable. For example, the music people like, or what they watch on TV.

3. Impact. What effect is a decision going to have? A life or death decision about cancer treatment is much more important than something trivial such as deciding whether or not to send someone a 10% discount voucher for frozen pizzas.

Bringing these three considerations together, it's when high impact decisions are being made, using immutable data, purely for the benefit of the decision maker, that the greatest ethical risks arise. Consequently, great care needs to be taken to ensure that the decision making system is fair, displays no unacceptable bias and hence, does not expose the decision maker to accusations of mis-behaviour. I'm not saying that an organization can't use high impact immutable data to further their own ends, but that they need be careful, and be ready to respond to challenges about the way they use that data.

If an organization identifies that it is using predictive analytics to take what are potentially "High risk" decisions, then what should it do? The answer is to take mitigating action as follows:

1. Try to identify at risk groups. The way to do this is to produce separate score distribution reports for groups such as women, ethnic minorities, children and so on. It can then be seen if there is any bias in the resulting scores; i.e. which groups tend to get lower than average scores (and will therefore be adversely treated compared to the wider population).

2. For those groups that score less well than the population average, constraints and over-ride rules should be used to ensure that they are treated in a fair way. Likewise, different cut-offs may need to be set for at risk groups.

3. Continue to monitor the situation once the decision making system goes live; i.e. regularly review the score profile and decision rules for key segments within the population. Cut-offs, constraints and over-rides should then be fine-tuned as required.

To illustrate this approach, let's think about an employment scenario. Consider a predictive model that is used to decide who to hire; i.e. a high score from the model indicates that the person is likely to be successful in the role, a low score less so. A concern might be that older men or people with young children are treated unfairly (which would potentially be in breach of EU law if the model was being used in this region). This is not to say that there isn't evidence that older men or people with children perform worse in their roles and would be worse hires than other people, but that it would be socially unacceptable and/or illegal to treat these groups differently. An ethically questionable system would be one where there was a single predictive model, and where a single cut-off score was applied to decide who to hire.

A more robust approach is to start by producing score distributions for older men and people with children. These are then compared against the score distribution for all potential hires. If necessary, separate cut-offs are then applied. This is to ensure that the proportion of people who are offered jobs in these two groups is the same as for the rest of the population.

Another similar approach is to construct separate models for each group. One model is built for the general population, one for older people and another for people with young children. Separate cut-off rules are then applied to each model to ensure that a consistent and aligned decision making strategy occurs.

Chapter 11. The Cutting Edge of Predictive Analytics

Predicting analytics is an exciting and evolving subject that is being driven by new developments in three areas:

1. **Models and Algorithms.** New approaches to predictive analytics are being developed all the time. One avenue of research is looking at new types of model. Another seeks to improve upon existing algorithms that produce scorecards, decision trees and so on, in order to improve the predictive accuracy of these types of model.

2. **Data.** Predictive models are only as good as the data used to build them. More/better data leads to better, more predictive models. This is one reason why "Big Data" and predictive analytics are so closely related.

3. **Systems and software.** The systems used to drive model development and deployment. The faster predictive models can be developed and deployed, the sooner the benefits can be realized.

Let's start by discussing the models and algorithms side of predictive analytics. Linear models and decision trees, which have been introduced in this book, are probably the most widely used types of predictive model in use today. However, if you talk to the young bucks in Silicon Valley, then they will probably laugh and then tell you that these types of model are somewhat "vintage" when it comes to predictive analytics – decision trees are *so* 1980s!

There are so many better types of predictive model out there these days…

In one sense this is true. Scorecards and decision trees are certainly not new. It's also the case that, on average, newer types of predictive model such as "neural networks", "support vector machines" and "ensembles", generate more accurate predictions than scorecards or decision trees.

Linear models and decision trees were first used commercially in the 1950s and 1960s, in an age when a typical computer was the size of a large desk and had less than 1% of the computational abilities of a basic smart phone today. Therefore, these simple types of predictive model could be developed and implemented relatively easily. Computer power is not really an issue these days, but simple models such as scorecards and decision trees remain very popular for the following reasons:

- **They are "White Box" in nature.** It's very easy to understand how a score, and hence a prediction about someone, is arrived at. Likewise, it's easy to see which data items contributed most significantly to the score, and which are less important.

- **They are easy to code.** Specialist software is not required to implement them. If resources are tight, then you can implement a scorecard or a decision tree as a small IT project, without needing to purchase additional hardware/software, and without needing to employ very expensive data scientists.

- **They still produce pretty good predictions.** Some predictive models are thousands of times more complex than a simple scorecard or decision tree. These advanced models are derived using "Artificial intelligence", "Pattern recognition" or "Deep learning" based techniques. However, even the most advanced predictive models tend to provide no more than a few percent uplift over simple scorecards or decision trees, and sometimes none at all.

What I want to make clear is that the big win for organizations is to make the leap to using automated decision making based on predictive analytics. The incremental benefits from using the most advanced methods available are more marginal.

If your organization does not currently use predictive analytics, then developing some simple models that can be integrated into your existing decision making infrastructure will give you most of the benefits. The fancy cutting edge stuff, which often requires specialist hardware and/or software, will provide greater benefits, but not a massive amount. Therefore don't delay. The 80/20 rules applies. You'll get 80% of the benefits for 20% of the effort.

It's also the case that if you can't get a simple predictive model to work, then just using a more complex approach, or buying some expensive hardware/software is unlikely to solve the underlying issues; i.e. the failure of a predictive analytics project is nearly always due to incorrect problem formulation, the underlying data or an organizational issue. The problem is unlikely to be due to the type of predictive model that has been developed.

OK. That's the argument for keeping faith with simple models such as scorecards and decision trees. However, if an organization is an established user of predictive analytics, and its predictive models are responsible for billions of dollars' worth of decisions each year, then there will be a drive to have they very best (most predictive) models possible – and with good reason. For a model responsible for a billion dollars' worth of decision making each year, then just a 0.1% uplift in performance equates to a $1m benefit. In this type of scenario it would be perfectly justifiable to employ a team of data scientists full-time to constantly challenge and improve upon the models that the organization employs.

The most advanced forms of predictive models in use today are ensemble models. With an ensemble, instead of having a single scorecard or decision tree, hundreds or possibly thousands of different models are constructed, each using a different data sample, and/or different algorithms to determine the model's parameters. Each model therefore makes predictions in a slightly different way. The scores (predictions) generated by each model will often be the same or very similar, but sometimes they will disagree with each other; i.e. some models will give some types of cases very high scores, whereas other models will give the same cases much lower scores and vice versa.

Using an ensemble model is a bit like having decisions made by a committee of experts rather than by a single expert. The reasons why the committee approach is better than having a single expert is twofold:

1. If one of the experts has specialist knowledge that the other's don't have, then this can be brought into the decision making process.

2. Some of the experts may, on occasion, make poor decisions. The other experts will use their collective knowledge to override (out vote) those cases.

Just like the committee, some of the models that form an ensemble will be particularly good at predicting the outcome of certain types of cases. Likewise, if any of the models are weak in certain areas (generate poor predictions) then these are overridden by the others.

Once constructed, the way an ensemble works is pretty straightforward. The score from each model is used to make a decision. A final decision is then made by simple majority vote. If we return to the heart disease scorecard model discussed earlier, then imagine that instead of a single scorecard, a thousand different scorecards are constructed. The original decision rule was to invite someone for a check-up if they scored 521 or more. With the ensemble, if at least 500 of the individual models generate a score of 521 or more, then the decision is to invite.

How much better are ensembles than single models? Sometimes none! However, in my experience it's not unusual for an ensemble to be around 5-10% better than a single model. If an insurance company found that using a decision tree resulted in a $40m reduction in claims over their previous manual process for the same amount of underwriting, then moving to an ensemble approach could reasonably be expected to provide an additional $2-4m benefit.

If all you are interested in is raw predictive accuracy, then ensembles are the way to go. If however, it's important for you to be able to explain how a model arrives at a given prediction, then you may want to think twice before going down the ensemble route because the solution will be much more complex and more difficult to understand than a single model approach.

Let's now move on to think about data. From reading the academic literature on predictive analytics, I would hazard a guess that 95% or more of it is about algorithms; i.e. very technical discussions about the cutting edge mathematical approaches that can squeeze a little bit more predictive accuracy from a given data set. In practice however, when it comes to improving the accuracy of predictive models, data is king.

Given a choice between a new algorithm for building a predictive model and having more/better data available, then data wins every time. To put it another way, very simple predictive models built using a good amount of high quality data always outperform more advanced approaches built using a smaller amount of lower quality data. If you really want to get more out of your predictive models, then improving the quality of the data used to build them, and seeking out new and better data sources, should come at the top of your priority list.

In the early days of Big Data[23], when the cost of data storage had fallen very dramatically in a short period of time, there was very much a "store and analyze it all" data philosophy amongst the pioneers. The message was that every organization should be gathering and analyzing all the data it could. Back then, there was a lot of talk about needing to invest in mass storage systems such as Hadoop. This was to allow organizations to store all the data that they could lay their hands on, in order to be able to produce the best predictive models possible, and hence gain a competitive advantage. However, the amount of data being generated has continued to increase year on year and shows no signs of slowing down. In fact, the volume of data is increasing at a far faster rate than the cost of data storage is falling.

This means that the benefit of having all available data to hand is to some extent offset by the costs of storing and analyzing all that data. As discussed previously, only a small fraction of all the data out there actually features in predictive models and is used to make predictions; i.e. once you know what types of data are predictive of how people are going to behave, then you can discard most of the other data because you don't need it. Continuing to maintain huge databases of "low value" data is not a very efficient use of time and resource.

These days, there are moves towards common data storage and aggregation – particularly when it comes to externally sourced data and data that is common across organizations. If people have ten apps on their phone supplied by ten different organizations, then it's very wasteful for each of those organizations to be gathering location and movement data themselves. It makes far more sense for one organization to manage the data, and then provide clients with the specific data items that are relevant to them.

If you look at companies such as Facebook, Google, Experian, Equifax and so forth, then this is exactly what they are doing. They undertake the hard work of collecting, formatting, preparing and summarizing data. They then package the useful bits and sell it on. In this way, individual organizations only acquire data that is genuinely useful to them. Consequently, they don't need to waste time and resources gathering huge amounts of data that they don't need.

The third driver of developments in predictive analytics is IT systems and software. As the volume of personal data has grown, and the frequency with which data changes has increased, so cycle times between model developments has reduced in many industries.

The traditional paradigm for developing and implementing predictive models is to separate these two parts of the process; i.e. develop your models first, and then implementation them. During the development phase, a data scientist spends days, weeks or even months gathering data and carrying out the statistical analysis required to build the model. When that part of the process is complete, there is a further exercise to code up the model within the production environment, test that the model works and then for it to be put into live operational use.

In many (and possibly most) industries this approach to predictive models is still applied and generally works pretty well. Not least, because after a model has been developed, it has to pass internal and external audit, and be subject to regulatory review before it can be put to use. This is important because if your entire business relies on the correct decisions being made, and you get it wrong, then the impact on the bottom line can be very considerable indeed.

For risk models in banking and insurance, for example, it can take a year or more between a predictive modelling project commencing and a model being implemented within the business. Every aspect of the model has to be fully documented, and then a cycle of discussion, feedback and further analysis needs to occur before the regulator signs-off the model as fit for use.

In other areas however, such as internet marketing, things move much faster. Data, and the relationships in that data, are changing frequently, some of it in real time. If an organization wants to retain a competitive edge then it needs a much more rapid cycle of model development and implementation. Models are rebuilt on a daily or more frequent basis in response to constant changes in the data. This has led to the development of IT systems that closely integrate the data an organization holds, the analytical tools used to create predictive models and the systems that deploy them.

These "In-database" systems stream data to predictive analytics tools without needing to extract the data first, drastically reducing the time required to pull data samples together, build predictive models and then to deploy those models operationally.

Once an in-database system has been configured, models can be redeveloped and deployed automatically. In theory, a new updated model can be constructed every time a new piece of data becomes available. New models are developed and deployed on a minute by minute basis. Consequently, it becomes impossible for a data scientist to be involved in the detail of every model that is constructed. Instead, the data scientist's role is to be part of the team the designs the wider system. In particular, they have responsibility for understanding the data the feeds the system, and how this maps to business problems that the system needs to create predictive models for.

After a system goes live, the software provides a dashboard for the data scientist that reports on the status of the overall system. For example, how well models within the system are performing, how model performance changes over time, how the data that feeds the analytics process is changing and so on.

The data scientists themselves only become involved in the detail when something goes awry, or when some new feature needs to be incorporated into the system. If there is an unexpected dip in model performance, then the data scientist will need to investigate and find out why model performance has declined. They will then instigate remedial action to correct the problem and return the system to optimal operating conditions.

A further focus of some of the newer predictive analytics software are intermediary tools which seek to provide a better interface between non-technical business users and the underlying data and algorithms required for predictive analytics.

The most advanced of these tools try to replace some of the tasks that would traditionally have been undertaken by data scientists. They can analyze and prepare data from different sources, apply a range of algorithms and present the results back to non-technical users in an easy to understand way without any formulas or equations. In particular, the software attempts to present results in a contextual way that makes business sense, rather than providing a more formal statistical perspective that data scientists are used to dealing with.

A prime example of this approach is the one taken by IBM with its Watson Analytics Software. The original version of Watson famously beat several human players in the general knowledge quiz show Jeopardy in the USA[24]. Watson has now evolved in to a commercial product. Behind the scenes, the software uses some very complex algorithms to extract information from a range of different data sources. The front end of the software is designed with managers and other business users in mind, rather than data scientists.

The net result is that when presented with suitable data, new insights and understanding about the behavior of customers can be presented to business users within hours, or even minutes, without the need to involve technical specialists in the process.

12. Concluding Remarks

First, I would like to thank you for taking the time to purchase and read this short introduction to the world of predictive analytics. I hope that you now have an understanding of what predictive analytics is, why it's important, and how it works.

If you liked the book, then please consider giving it a positive review on Amazon, Goodreads or other review sites. You may also like my full length book:

• **Predictive Analytics, Data Mining and Big Data. Myths, Misconceptions and Methods.**

Which is published by Palgrave Macmillan. It's written in a similar style and covers similar ground, but in greater detail. The book is available at Amazon and all good bookstores.

If on the other hand, you felt the book didn't fill the 56 minute void in your life that you were expecting it too, then I'm sorry to hear that. Please feel free to drop me a line to let me know why at: steve.finlay@virginmedia.com. Likewise, if you have any positive feedback, I'll be very happy to receive that too.

Steven Finlay

15th July 2015

Appendix A. Evaluating Predictive Models

Once a predictive model has been constructed it needs to be assessed to determine how well it predicts behaviour. Sometimes there is a single cut-off score that results in the business objective being met, which can be established by looking at the score distribution table (such as those in Figures 3, 4 and 6). However, in many situations there is not one obvious cut-off score to choose. There is a range of possible cut-offs, any one of which meets the business objective, but with different benefits and drawbacks. Likewise, common practice is to build several different predictive models. The performance of the models are then compared against each other so that the best one can be chosen.

If you think back to the heart disease case study, used throughout this book, then you will remember that we looked at a decision tree model and a scorecard model. Both models provided solutions that met the business objective as stated; i.e. identify at least 50% of people who will develop heart disease, but invite no more than 5% of the entire population for a check-up. However, the scorecard model performed better overall. This is because it identified 62% of cases within the highest scoring 5% whereas the decision tree only identified 55%

In a similar vein, one could argue that both models over delivered. They identified more than the required 50% of cases. What this means is that there is actually some flexibility in how the cut-off is chosen; i.e. there is more than one cut-off that meets the objective. Two possible ways in which the model could be used are:

1. **Maximize outcomes.** Choose the cut-off which results in exactly 5% of the population being invited for a check-up; i.e. use all available resources. This will result in more than 50% of heart disease cases being identified (this is the answer presented previously in the case study; i.e. the 521 cut-off score for the scorecard or the 12 cut-off score for the decision tree).

2. **Minimize resources.** Choose the cut-off which results in exactly 50% of heart disease cases being invited for a check-up. This means that less than 5% of the population will be invited for a check-up because a cut-off score above 521 would be chosen.

Which option to choose depends on what's most important to the health authority. If it wants to maximize the identification of heart disease, then option 1 is best. If it wants to minimize resource, then option 2 is better. The health authority could of course, also choose a cut-off score that lies somewhere between these two.

More generally, in these types of situations there are two considerations when choosing cut-offs:

- **Purity (Lift).** If a high cut-off is chosen, then only a few cases will be selected, but of those selected, a high proportion will display the characteristic you are interested in.

- **Volume (Gain).** If a lower cut-off is chosen, then more cases will be selected, and overall more cases of interest will be within the selected group (those above the cut-off). However, the purity of selected cases will fall; i.e. a lower proportion of those above the cut-off will display the characteristic you are interested in.

To help decide on cut-off strategies and the trade-off between purity and volume, two popular tools that are used to assess the impact of different cut-off strategies are Lift Charts and Gains charts. These provide an easy to use visual representation of how a model performs. A lift chart gives a view of purity. Figure 7 provides an example of a Lift Chart for the heart disease scorecard that was presented in Figure 2.

Figure 7. A lift chart for the heart disease scorecard.

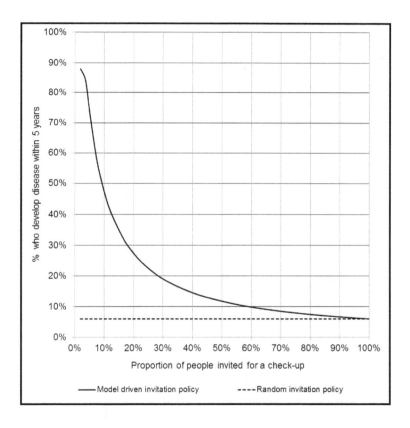

In Figure 7, the X axis shows the proportion of people invited for a check-up. The Y axis shows the proportion of those who are invited, who can be expected to develop the disease. The dotted straight line is the base rate. The base rate is the percentage of people expected to develop heart disease over the next 5 years within the population at large i.e. 6%. To put it another way, the base rate represents a random selection strategy for inviting people for check-ups.

The solid curved line shows what would happen if the prioritization process for deciding who to invite for a check-up was based on the scores from the scorecard. For example, the graph shows that if the highest scoring 40% of the population are invited for a check-up, then about 15% of these would develop heart disease. If volumes were reduced and say, only 10% were invited for a check-up, then the proportion (purity) would rise to around 50%

The smaller the proportion targeted for medical intervention, the higher the proportion with the disease. To put it another way, if you only target the small number of people in the population with the very highest scores, then one can expect a very high proportion of those selected to have heart disease. If the invited group is enlarged however, by including people with lower scores, then overall the proportion identified (the purity) will fall.

The lift chart is therefore a way of comparing trade-offs between volume and purity.

How has the Lift Chart been produced? Figure 8 shows an extended version of the Score distribution table for the heart disease scorecard that was introduced in Figure 3.

Figure 8. Extended score distribution table.

Score range From	Score range To	Number of people	% of population	Number with heart disease after 5 yrs.	% with heart disease after 5 yrs.	Descending cumulative Number of people	Descending cumulative % of population	Descending cumulative Number with heart disease after 5 yrs.	Descending cumulative % with heart disease after 5 yrs.	Purity (Lift)
0	300	55,950	11.19%	40	0.07%	500,000	100.00%	30,000	6.00%	6.00%
301	320	56,606	11.32%	68	0.12%	444,050	88.81%	29,960	6.75%	6.75%
321	340	59,700	11.94%	129	0.22%	387,444	77.49%	29,892	7.72%	7.72%
341	360	58,706	11.74%	216	0.37%	327,744	65.55%	29,763	9.08%	9.08%
361	380	64,429	12.89%	403	0.63%	269,038	53.81%	29,547	10.98%	10.98%
381	400	52,749	10.55%	575	1.09%	204,609	40.92%	29,144	14.24%	14.24%
401	420	34,089	6.82%	600	1.76%	151,860	30.37%	28,569	18.81%	18.81%
421	440	21,107	4.22%	632	2.99%	117,771	23.55%	27,969	23.75%	23.75%
441	460	17,269	3.45%	878	5.09%	96,664	19.33%	27,337	28.28%	28.28%
461	480	23,364	4.67%	2,020	8.65%	79,395	15.88%	26,459	33.33%	33.33%
481	500	17,477	3.50%	2,553	14.61%	56,031	11.21%	24,439	43.62%	43.62%
501	520	13,554	2.71%	3,366	24.84%	38,554	7.71%	21,885	56.77%	56.77%
521	540	7,103	1.42%	3,463	48.76%	25,000	5.00%	18,519	74.08%	74.08%
541	560	8,260	1.65%	6,587	79.74%	17,897	3.58%	15,056	84.12%	84.12%
561	999	9,637	1.93%	8,469	87.88%	9,637	1.93%	8,469	87.88%	87.88%
		500,000		30,000	6.0%					

The first four of the extra columns on the right in Figure 8 show descending cumulative figures; i.e. they show the number and proportion of cases scoring at or above a given score. The lift (rightmost column) is calculated by dividing the cumulative number of people with heart disease by the cumulative total. For example, the lift at a score of 501 is calculated as:

$$Lift = 21{,}885 \: / \: 38{,}554 = 56.77\%$$

Which means that 56.77% of those scoring above 501 are expected to develop heart disease. The lift chart is then created by plotting the cumulative % of population column against the lift.

A Lift Chart provides a purity perspective on the population across the range of possible cut-off scores. A Gains Chart on the other hand is used to provide a volume orientated view. Figure 9 shows the Gains chart for the heart disease scorecard.

The gains chart has been produced by plotting the cumulative percentage of the total population at or above the score, against the cumulative proportion of heart disease cases at or above the same score; i.e. the second and fourth rightmost columns in Figure 8. For example, in Figure 9 it can be seen that if one invites 10% of the population for a check-up, then that will result in about 80% of all heart disease cases in the population being included on the invite list. Similarly, if one invites 30% of the population, then approximately 95% of all cases will be on the invite list.

Figure 9. A Gain chart for the heart disease scorecard.

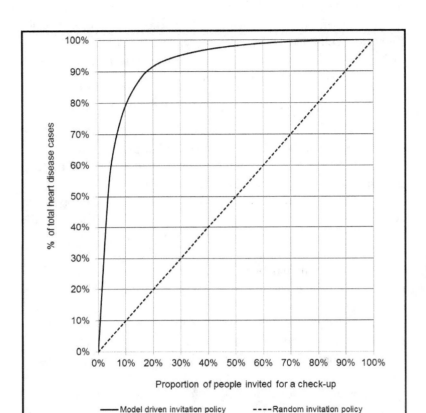

Lift and gains charts are very useful tools that can be produced for any type of classification model to help business users decide how models should be used. Similar graphs can also be produced for regression type models.

Data scientists will also use specific metrics to measure how good the overall predictive accuracy of a model is. Perhaps the three most popular measures that are used to do this are:

- **AUC (area under the curve).** This is a popular measure for evaluating classification models. AUC ranges from 0.5 to 1. A value of 0.5 indicates that a model has no predictive ability; i.e. is useless. A value of 1.0 indicates a perfect predictor that gets it right every time. The GINI statistic and Somers'D are similar measures[25].

- **Percentage correctly classified (PCC).** This is simply the proportion of events that are correctly classified for a given cut-off score. If an event scores above the cut-off score, then the model predicts correctly. Likewise, if a non-event occurs and it scores below the cut-off then the model has also got it right. For the heart disease scorecard with a cut-off of 521 the proportion of cases correctly classified was 96.4%

- **(Adjusted) R-squared.** This is the most popular measure for evaluating regression models. It is based on the differences between the actual and predicted values for each observation in the development sample. An R-squared value of zero indicates that a model has no predictive ability; i.e. is useless. A value of 1 indicates a perfect predictor that gets it spot on every time.

Measures such as Adjusted R-squared, AUC and PCC are used to compare the performance of different models, and to assess how model performance changes over time. When a new classification model is built, the performance of the old and new models are compared to see how much better the new model is. Likewise, if two or more different types of model are developed for a given problem, then the one with the highest AUC, PCC, R-Squared and so on will be deemed to be the best; i.e. the most predictive.

There are literally dozens of other metrics that people have developed to measure how well models perform, but AUC and PCC are by far the most popular metrics for assessing the performance of classification models, and Adjusted R-Squared is the most popular measure for assessing regression models.

If you want to learn more about these and other measures for assessing predictive models, then there are a host of online resources available, including a large number of Wikipedia entries.

Appendix B. Further Information and Recommended Reading

The following are some of the primary internet resources for predictive analytics and related technologies (Big data, data mining, machine learning, etc.)

Operational Database Management Systems. http://www.odbms.org/ This site is supported by a range of industry experts. It covers a wide range of topics relating to the implementation and application of new technologies associated with predictive analytics, cloud computing and Big Data, amongst other things.

KDnuggets. http://www.kdnuggets.com/ This is one of the leading sites providing resources for data scientists.

AnalyticBridge. http://www.analyticbridge.com/ AnalyticBridge hosts a range of articles, blogs and discussion forums about predictive analytics that is open to all. There is a broad range of topics covered, from the strategic to the very technical / operational.

LinkedIn. http://www.linkedin.com/ There are several forums on LinkedIn that discuss predictive analytics and related topics.

StatSoft. http://www.statsoft.com/Textbook. This is a website managed by Dell, providers of the STATISTICA statistical software package. If you want to know more about a wide range of statistical methods, including those used in predictive analytics, then this is a great site to refer to.

The following is a list of books that are suitable for the general reader; i.e. no formulas or tech speak.

Davenport, T., Kim, J. (2013). *Keeping Up with the Quants: Your Guide to Understanding and Using Analytics.* **Harvard Business Review Press.** Davenport was one of the first people to write an accessible analytics text in his 2006 book – Competing on Analytics. This new book is written specifically for non-technical managers to help them understand and work with technically minded people who do predictive analytics; i.e. data scientists.

Finlay, S. (2014). *Predictive Analytics, Data Mining and Big Data. Myths, Misconceptions and Methods.* **Palgrave Macmillan.** This is one of my books, so I'm bound to say nice things about it. Primarily it's a book about predictive analytics, but it also provides a brief introduction to Big Data. The main focus is on practical issues around the development and implementation of predictive models.

Kahneman, D. (2012). *Thinking, Fast and Slow.* **Penguin.** This is a book about decision making. It digs into the reasons why people make decisions in the way that they do. In particular, it discusses why people often have trouble accepting automated decision making systems, based on predictive analytics. However, the book is much broader than this. It discusses a wide range of issues associated with human decision making processes.

Siegel, E. (2013). *Predictive Analytics: the Power to Predict Who Will Click, Buy, Lie, or Die.* **Wiley.** Very much a marmite book. You'll either love it or hate it, but it's the book that brought predictive analytics to the attention of a much wider audience than ever before. I like marmite!

Silver, N. (2012). *The Signal and the Noise: Why So Many Predictions Fail.* **Penguin.** This is not really a predictive analytics book. However, what is very relevant is the focus on understanding why so many forecasting systems fail. It discusses why more attention needs to focus on the weaknesses and pitfalls of forecasting and prediction, so as to improve the quality of forecasting models in the future.

If you want to tool up and get a bit more into the technical aspects of predictive analytics, then I recommend the following:

Baesens, B. (2014). *Analytics in a Big Data World: The Essential Guide to Data Science and its Applications.* **Wiley.** This book provides clear descriptions of all the key stages involved in developing a predictive model. A great read for those with a little bit of mathematical and/or statistical knowledge, but you don't need a higher degree in mathematics or statistics to understand the concepts that Baesens puts forward.

Bishop, C. M. (2007). *Pattern Recognition and Machine Learning* **(Information Science and Statistics). Springer.** This book covers a lot of the theoretical material underpinning many of the tools commonly used for data mining and predictive analytics.

Bishop, C. M. (1995). *Neural Networks for Pattern Recognition.* **Clarendon Press.** It has been more than twenty years since its original publication, yet this remains one of the few definitive guides to the theory and application of neural networks.

Crawley, M. (2012). *The R Book. 2nd Edition.* **Wiley.** There are lots of statistical packages that can be used to construct predictive models. However, R is probably the most popular. R is open source and can be downloaded for free from the CRAN website http://cran.r-project.org/ If you already have some programming knowledge then this book provides a comprehensive introduction to the R language.

Easley, D. and Kleinberg, J. (2010). *Networks, Crowds, and Markets: Reasoning About a Highly Connected World.* **Cambridge University Press.** I've not discussed social network analysis in the main part of the text, but social networks are a very important source of data for many types of predictive models. Companies like Facebook, Google and LinkedIn, apply predictive analytics to the data they hold to drive their advertising and target marketing activities. This book provides a blend of practical and theoretical material about the application of social network analysis in a number of environments.

Hastie, T., Tibshirani, R. and Friedman, J. (2011). *The Elements of Statistical Learning: Data Mining, Inference, and Prediction, 2nd Edition.* **Springer.** A detailed and technical guide to many of the data mining tools used in predictive analytics, written by three of the world's leading academics in the field.

Hosmer, D. and Lemeshow, S. (2013). *Applied Logistic Regression* **(Wiley Series in Probability and Statistics). 3rd Edition Wiley.** Logistic regression remains one of the most popular and widely used methods for generating predictive models. This is the first book I recommend to people who want to know more about this method.

Khun, M.(2013), Johnson, K. *Applied Predictive Modeling.* **Springer.** Another well-constructed book in a similar vein to Baesens (above). It combines practical advice with the more mathematical aspects of the subject.

Linoff, G. S. and Berry, M. J. (2011). *Data Mining Techniques: For Marketing, Sales, and Customer Relationship Management.* **3rd. Edition. Wiley.** This is a broad, well-rounded, and not overtly technical book that describes the most popular data mining techniques applied to direct marketing.

Witten, I. H., Frank, E. and Hall, M. A. (2011). *Data Mining: Practical Machine Learning Tools and Techniques, 3rd Edition (The Morgan Kaufmann Series in Data Management Systems).* **Morgan Kaufmann.** This is a detailed reference manual for those interested in practical data mining. I found it provided a nice blend of theory and practice, with many good examples.

Appendix C. Popular Terms in Predictive Analytics

Algorithm. An algorithm is a set of instructions or procedures, executed in sequence to solve a particular problem. In predictive analytics, various algorithms are applied to discover patterns in data and to create predictive models.

Big Data. A very large collection of varied, changeable data, which is difficult to process using a standard PC/Server; i.e. typically terabytes in size or larger. Big data technologies make use of advanced computer architectures and specialist software to facilitate the rapid processing of these data sets. Predictive Analytics is one of the primary tools used to extract value from Big Data.

Causation. The reasoning behind why something happened. Not to be confused with correlation.

Classification model. A predictive model which predicts if a given event will or will not occur. For example, the likelihood that two people will hit it off on a date, the probability that someone will buy a certain type of car, or the chance that a person develops diabetes sometime in the next 10 years. The score generated by a classification model is an estimate of the likelihood of the event occurring. Not to be confused with regression model.

Cluster. Clusters are groups that contain people or things with similar traits. For example, people with similar ages and incomes might be in one cluster, those with similar job roles and family sizes in another.

Correlation. One variable is correlated with another if a change in that variable occurs in tandem with a change in another. It is important to appreciate that this does not necessarily mean that one thing is caused by another. Stork migration is correlated with births (more children born in the spring when storks migrate), but stork migration does not cause births!

Cut-off score (Score based decision rule). Most predictive models generate a score. Cut-off scores are used to decide how people are treated on the basis of the score. Those who score above the cut-off receive one treatment, those scoring below the cut-off another. For example, when assessing people for a medical condition, only those scoring above the cut-off; i.e. those with the highest risk of developing the condition, are offered treatment.

Data mining. Data mining is the science of finding useful information in data sets that a human being would be unable to identify easily by casting their eye over it. Data mining makes use of a wide range of algorithms and automated procedures taken from various disciplines which include statistics, computing and artificial intelligence/machine learning.

Data scientist. The name given to someone who can combine mathematical knowledge with data and IT skills in a pragmatic way, to deliver practical value add predictive analytics based solutions. Good data scientists focus on delivering useful solutions that work in real world environments. They don't get too hung up on theory. If it works it works!

Decision tree. A type of predictive model, created using an algorithm that recursively segments a population into smaller and smaller groups. Also known as a Classification and Regression Tree (Because they can be used for both classification and regression!)

Deep learning. Predictive models based on complex neural networks (or related architectures), containing very large numbers of neurons and many hidden layers and/or complex overlapping networks. These tools are proving successful at complex "AI" type problems such as object recognition and language translation.

Development sample. The set of data used by the predictive analytics process to construct a predictive model. Development samples need to contain at least several hundred cases, but usually larger samples, containing thousands or millions of cases, are used.

Ensemble. A predictive model comprised of several subsidiary models (as few as 3 or sometimes many thousands). All of the subsidiary models predict the same outcome, but have been constructed using different methods and/or using different data. This means that the models don't always generate the same predictions. The ensemble combines all of the individual predictions to arrive at a final prediction. Model ensembles often (but not always) significantly outperform the best individual model.

Forecast horizon. Most (but not all) predictive models forecast future unknown events or quantities. The forecast horizon is the time frame over which a model predicts. For example, marketing models typically predict response over a forecast horizon of hours or days. In medicine, forecast horizons of many years are used when predicting survival probabilities for particular conditions.

Gains chart. A commonly used visual tool used to demonstrate the benefits of a model. Often used in conjunction with a lift chart.

Hadoop. A data storage solution that makes use of lots of cheap "off the shelf" PCs to store and process massive amounts of data.

Lift chart. A widely used graphical tool for demonstrating the practical benefits of a predictive model. Often used in conjunction with a Gains chart.

Linear model. A popular type of predictive model that is easy to understand and use. A score is calculated by multiplying the value of each characteristic by its relevant weight, and then summing up all the results. A popular way of representing linear models is in the form of a scorecard (see below).

Linear regression. One of the oldest and most popular methods for creating regression models. The development of linear regression dates back more than 100 years.

Logistic regression. A very simple and popular method used for creating classification models.

Machine learning. Machine learning is often considered to be a sub-set of data mining. Machine learning algorithms derive from research into artificial intelligence and pattern recognition. The algorithms used to train neural networks and support vector machines are two examples of machine learning approaches.

MapReduce. A programming approach which enables data stored on Hadoop (and other Big Data platforms) to be processed very quickly. MapReduce works by splitting data processing tasks into lots of smaller sub-tasks that can then be implemented in parallel across the network of PCs that comprise a Hadoop network.

Model, see predictive model.

Monitoring. The performance of predictive models tends to deteriorate over time. It is therefore prudent to instigate a monitoring regime following model implementation to measure how models are performing on an ongoing basis. Models are redeveloped when the monitoring indicates that a significant deterioration in model performance has occurred.

Neural network. A popular type of model derived using machine learning algorithms. Neural networks are well suited to capturing complex interactions and non-linarites in data in a way that is analogous to human learning. "Deep" neural networks (Deep learning/Deep belief networks) are very large and complex neural networks (containing thousands or millions of artificial neurons) that are used for "AI" tasks such as object recognition and language translation.

Neuron. The key component of a neural network, which is often discussed as being analogous to biological neurons in the human brain. In reality, a neuron is a linear model, whose score is then subject to a (non-linear) transformation. A neural network can therefore be considered as a set of interconnected linear models and non-linear transformations.

Odds. A way to represent the likelihood of an event occurring. The odds of an event is equal to $(1/p) - 1$ where p is the probability of the event. Likewise, the probability is equal to $(1/Odds+1)$. So, odds of 1:1 is the same as a probability of 0.5, odds of 2:1 a probability of 0.33, 3:1 a probability of 0.25 and so on.

Over-fitting. The bane of a data scientist's life. Over-fitting occurs when an algorithm goes too far in its search for correlations in the data used to develop a predictive model. The net result is that the model looks to be very predictive when measured against the development sample, but performs very poorly when it's used to predict new outcomes using data that has not been presented to the model before.

Over-ride rule. Sometimes, certain actions must be taken regardless of the prediction generated by a model. For example, a predictive model used to target people with offers for beer might predict that some children are very likely to take up the offer. An override rule is therefore put in place to prevent offers being sent to children, regardless of the score generated by the model.

Predictive model. A predictive model is the output from the predictive analytics process. The model captures the relationships (correlations) that the process has discovered. Once a predictive model has been created, it can then be applied to new situations to predict what people are likely to do in the future.

Random forest. Random forests are an ensemble method, based on combining together the output of a large number of decisions trees, where each decision tree has been created under a slightly different set of conditions. Random forests are one of the most successful and widely applied ensemble methods.

Regression model. A popular tool for predicting the magnitude of something. For example, how much someone will spend or how long they will live. This is in contrast to a classification model which predicts the likelihood of an event occurring.

Response (choice) modeling. This term refers to marketing models used to predict the likelihood that someone buys a product or service that they have been targeted with. A response model is a type of classification model.

Score. Most predictions generated by predictive models are represented in the form of a single number (a score). For a classification model the score is a representation of the probability of an event occurring e.g. how likely someone is to respond to a marketing communication or the probability of them defaulting on a loan. For a regression model the score represents the magnitude of the predicted behaviour e.g. how much someone might spend, or how long they might live.

Scorecard. A scorecard is a way of presenting linear models which is easy for non-experts to understand. The main benefit of a scorecard is that it is additive; i.e. a model score is calculated by simply adding up the points that apply. There is no multiplication, division or other more complex arithmetic.

Score distribution. A table or graph showing how the scores from a predictive model are distributed across the population of interest. Lift and Gain charts are both ways of presenting the score distribution in a graphical form.

Sentiment analysis. This is a popular technique for extracting information about peoples' attitude towards things. For example, if they had a positive or negative experience when using a particular product or service. In predictive analytics, sentiment analysis is used to extract information from text or speech that is then used to build predictive models.

Support vector machine. An advanced type of non-linear model. Support vector machines have some similarities with neural networks.

Validation sample. An independent data set used to evaluate a predictive model after it has been constructed. The validation sample should be completely separate from the development sample, and should not be used during model construction. Using one (or more) validation samples is important, because predictive analytics sometimes over-fits a model to the development sample. This means that if you evaluate a predictive model using the development sample, it can appear to be more predictive than it actually is.

Notes

[1] People usually talk about predictive analytics as something that predicts future events. However, strictly speaking, the event simply has to be unknown. The unknown event can be in the past, present or future. For example, predictive analytics can be applied to estimate people's current income if it's unknown. The predicted income is then used to drive marketing offers; i.e. target those with high predicted incomes.

[2] The original role of credit reference agencies (also known as credit reporting agencies or credit bureaus) was as a central repository for data about debts and loan repayments. This is still at the core of what they do, but these days credit reference agencies hold all sorts of other personal information. Consequently, a credit report can contain a wide variety of personal data, in addition to information about a person's credit history. Credit reference agencies were arguably the first "Big Data" companies, decades before the term began to be applied to the likes of Google, Amazon, Facebook, et al.

[3] Predicting consumer behaviour is perhaps the most common application of predictive analytics, but there are others. For example, the same type of techniques are used to predict stock prices, when complex machines are likely to breakdown and which organizations are likely to go bankrupt in the next year.

[4] Siegel, E. (2013). Predictive Analytics: The Power to Predict Who Will Click, Buy, Lie, or Die. Wiley.

[5] Many, but not all credit scores are scaled in this way. More formally, the "standard" scaling for credit scoring models is for a score of 500 to equate to a 50% chance of being a good payer (odds of 1:1). The odds then double every 20 points. A score of 520 means 2:1 odds of being a good repayer (66% Chance of repaying the loan) , a score of 540 odds of 4:1 (80% chance of repaying the loan) and so on.

[6] There are lots of different types of heart disease with different causes and symptoms, but for the sake of simplicity we'll consider heart disease as a single condition for this example.

[7] Body Mass Index (BMI) is calculated as a person's weight in kilograms divided by their height in metres squared. For someone who is 180cm tall and weighs 80kg their body mass index is: $80/(1.8 * 1.8) = 24.69$. In the UK, a BMI of 19-25 is considered normal. A BMI under 19 indicates a person may be underweight. 25-30 indicates that someone is likely to be overweight, and more than 30 obese. Note that BMI is only a guide, and other factors such as build, age and muscle mass are important. Some athletes would be classified as overweight using BMI, due to having more than the average amount of muscle mass.

[8] People have been doing data science type roles for decades under the

guise of "management science", "operational research" and other job titles, but "data scientist" is the popular term that seems to have become attached to these types of roles since the early 2010s.

[9] There are lots of algorithms that can be applied to generate scorecards, but the most popular method is called "Logistic regression." Other popular approaches include genetic algorithms, linear programming and discriminant analysis (linear regression).

[10] Using a new sample of data to evaluate a predictive model is important when evaluating how good the model is. This is because when predictive models are constructed a major concern is a problem called **Over-fitting**. Over-fitting means that the predictive analytics process has been over-optimistic. It finds relationships in the development sample that don't exist in the wider population. This means that when a predictive model is being evaluated, it's always wise to use a validation sample to measure the model's performance. The validation sample should be a completely independent sample that was not used to construct the model.

[11] The minimum possible score for this model is 281. The maximum possible score is 605.

[12] Calculated as: 1 / 0.0176.

[13] Note that this is an artificial example and not a genuine model developed for use by health practitioners. Therefore, you should not take the predictions generated by the model to be a true representation of your (or anyone else's) chance of developing heart disease.

[14] In practice, several validation samples would be taken (rather than just one). At least one of these would be an "out of time" sample, from a different time period to the development sample. If the results from the various validation samples tell a similar tale, then that is usually sufficient to indicate that the model will work as intended; i.e. that its predictive performance and accuracy will be similar to that observed from the validation / out of time samples.

[15] This is generally true, but not universally true. There are occasionally problems where one particular type of model or algorithm is significantly better/worse than another. Generally, its good practice to build a few different types of model to see if this is the case or not.

[16] For example, the individual in question had moved overseas and was therefore beyond the reach of the tax authorities. Likewise, the system often identified people who had become bankrupt. Even though these people technically owe a lot of tax, the tax is uncollectable due to the bankruptcy, which has resulted in the person's debts being written off by the courts.

[17] The exception to this is where a predictive model is being constructed

as a proof of concept. For example, a data scientist may be employed to see if building a predictive model is feasible, and would do some experimental model building to see if the project is viable. After all, the last thing you would want to do is build a full end-to-end IT and decision making infrastructure for predictive analytics, and then find out that you can't use it!

[18] In situations like this, it would probably be possible to derive some type of mapping between net and gross income. However, gross and net income are not always well correlated and depend to some extent on previous tax history, family situation and sources of income.

[19] In a strict sense, Big Data covers more than just data about people. The term is also applied to very large amounts of data about processes or systems. For example, climate change data, satellite imaging data, traffic data, the data generated by a manufacturing plant and so on.

[20] Of course, that is not how it was. Life was just as hard, but the problems were different; i.e. huge amounts of time were spent trying to find clever solutions to maximize limited storage and optimize the very limited processing power available at that time. Likewise, the software available for predictive analytics was far more limited than what is available today.

[21] Predictive analytics (and most other data related tasks) requires data to be in numeric or categorical format. Therefore, a key data processing task is to transform all of the data in to this format. For example, creating yes/no indicators to represent positive or negative sentiments expressed in the a piece of text, or counters to record the number of times certain words or phrases appear.

[22] For example, see the following meta-study: Orlitzky, M., Schmidt, F. L., Rynes, S. L. (2003). Corporate Social and Financial Performance: A Meta-analysis. Organization Studies, volume 24, number 3, pages 403-441.

[23] Big Data first entered the popular vernacular in around 2010/11.

[24] http://www.bbc.co.uk/news/technology-12491688

[25] In theory, there are cases where the AUC can be less than 0.5. However, in practice, that tends to indicate some underlying problem with the way the model has been built, rather than a true representation of the model's performance.

www.ingramcontent.com/pod-product-compliance
Lightning Source LLC
Chambersburg PA
CBHW060948050326
40689CB00012B/2599